T0196102

MACAT

An Analysis of

Edward Said's

Orientalism

Riley Quinn

ROUTLEDGE

Published by Macat International Ltd
24:13 Coda Centre, 189 Munster Road, London SW6 6AW.

Distributed exclusively by Routledge
2 Park Square, Milton Park, Abingdon, Oxon OX14 4RN
711 Third Avenue, New York, NY 10017, USA

Routledge is an imprint of the Taylor & Francis Group, an informa business

www.macat.com
info@macat.com

Cataloguing in Publication Data
A catalogue record for this book is available from the British Library.
Library of Congress Cataloguing-in-Publication Data is available upon request.
Cover illustration: Etienne Gilfillan

ISBN 978-1-912302-92-5 (hardback)
ISBN 978-1-912127-94-8 (paperback)
ISBN 978-1-912281-80-0 (e-book)

Notice
The information in this book is designed to orientate readers of the work under analysis,
to elucidate and contextualise its key ideas and themes, and to aid in the development
of critical thinking skills. It is not meant to be used, nor should it be used, as a
substitute for original thinking or in place of original writing or research. References and
notes are provided for informational purposes and their presence does not constitute
endorsement of the information or opinions therein. This book is presented solely for
educational purposes. It is sold on the understanding that the publisher is not engaged
to provide any scholarly advice. The publisher has made every effort to ensure that
this book is accurate and up-to-date, but makes no warranties or representations with
regard to the completeness or reliability of the information it contains. The information
and the opinions provided herein are not guaranteed or warranted to produce particular
results and may not be suitable for students of every ability. The publisher shall not be
liable for any loss, damage or disruption arising from any errors or omissions, or from
the use of this book, including, but not limited to, special, incidental, consequential or
other damages caused, or alleged to have been caused, directly or indirectly, by the
information contained within.

CONTENTS

WAYS IN TO THE TEXT

Who Was Edward Said?   9

What Does *Orientalism* Say?   11

Why Does *Orientalism* Matter?   11

SECTION 1: INFLUENCES

Module 1: The Author and the Historical Context   14

Module 2: Academic Context   20

Module 3: The Problem   25

Module 4: The Author's Contribution   30

SECTION 2: IDEAS

Module 5: Main Ideas   35

Module 6: Secondary Ideas   41

Module 7: Achievement   45

Module 8: Place in the Author's Work   50

SECTION 3: IMPACT

Module 9: The First Responses   56

Module 10: The Evolving Debate   61

Module 11: Impact and Influence Today   68

Module 12: Where Next?   72

Glossary of Terms   78

People Mentioned in the Text   87

Works Cited   97

THE MACAT LIBRARY

The Macat Library is a series of unique academic explorations of seminal works in the humanities and social sciences – books and papers that have had a significant and widely recognised impact on their disciplines. It has been created to serve as much more than just a summary of what lies between the covers of a great book. It illuminates and explores the influences on, ideas of, and impact of that book. Our goal is to offer a learning resource that encourages critical thinking and fosters a better, deeper understanding of important ideas.

Each publication is divided into three Sections: Influences, Ideas, and Impact. Each Section has four Modules. These explore every important facet of the work, and the responses to it.

This Section-Module structure makes a Macat Library book easy to use, but it has another important feature. Because each Macat book is written to the same format, it is possible (and encouraged!) to cross-reference multiple Macat books along the same lines of inquiry or research. This allows the reader to open up interesting interdisciplinary pathways.

To further aid your reading, lists of glossary terms and people mentioned are included at the end of this book (these are indicated by an asterisk [*] throughout) – as well as a list of works cited.

Macat has worked with the University of Cambridge to identify the elements of critical thinking and understand the ways in which six different skills combine to enable effective thinking.
Three allow us to fully understand a problem; three more give us the tools to solve it. Together, these six skills make up the **PACIER** model of critical thinking. They are:

ANALYSIS – understanding how an argument is built
EVALUATION – exploring the strengths and weaknesses of an argument
INTERPRETATION – understanding issues of meaning

CREATIVE THINKING – coming up with new ideas and fresh connections
PROBLEM-SOLVING – producing strong solutions
REASONING – creating strong arguments

To find out more, visit **WWW.MACAT.COM**.

CRITICAL THINKING AND *ORIENTALISM*

Primary critical thinking skill: INTERPRETATION
Secondary critical thinking skill: ANALYSIS

Edward Said's *Orientalism* is a masterclass in the art of interpretation wedded to close analysis. Interpretation is characterized by careful attention to the meanings of terms, by clarifying, questioning definitions, and positing clear definitions. Combined with one of the main sub-skills of analysis – drawing inferences and finding implicit reasons and assumptions in arguments – it becomes a powerful tool for critical thought.

In *Orientalism*, the theorist, critic and cultural historian Edward Said uses interpretation and analysis to closely examine Western representations of the "Orient" and ask what they are really doing, and why. One of his central arguments is that Western representations of the East and Middle East persistently define it as "other," setting it up in opposition to the West. Through careful analysis of a range of texts and other materials, Said shows that implicit assumptions about the "Orient's" otherness underlie much Western thought and writing about it. Clarifying consistently the differences between the real-world East and the constructed ideas of the "Orient", these interpretative skills power his analysis, and provide the basis for an argument that has proven hugely influential in literary criticism, philosophy, and even politics.

ABOUT THE AUTHOR OF THE ORIGINAL WORK

The cultural critic and public intellectual **Edward Said** (1935–2003) was born in Jerusalem, in what was then British-governed Palestine. He was raised there and in Cairo, where his family moved following the Arab-Israeli war of 1948. A brilliant student, Said concluded a somewhat turbulent education with a PhD in English Literature at Harvard University in 1964. Settling in the United States until his death, Said spent the remainder of his academic career at Columbia University. His major contribution to the humanities was his significant role in defining the field of postcolonial studies.

ABOUT THE AUTHOR OF THE ANALYSIS

Riley Quinn holds master's degrees in politics and international relations from both LSE and the University of Oxford.

ABOUT MACAT

GREAT WORKS FOR CRITICAL THINKING

Macat is focused on making the ideas of the world's great thinkers accessible and comprehensible to everybody, everywhere, in ways that promote the development of enhanced critical thinking skills.

It works with leading academics from the world's top universities to produce new analyses that focus on the ideas and the impact of the most influential works ever written across a wide variety of academic disciplines. Each of the works that sit at the heart of its growing library is an enduring example of great thinking. But by setting them in context – and looking at the influences that shaped their authors, as well as the responses they provoked – Macat encourages readers to look at these classics and game-changers with fresh eyes. Readers learn to think, engage and challenge their ideas, rather than simply accepting them.

'Macat offers an amazing first-of-its-kind tool for interdisciplinary learning and research. Its focus on works that transformed their disciplines and its rigorous approach, drawing on the world's leading experts and educational institutions, opens up a world-class education to anyone.'

Andreas Schleicher
Director for Education and Skills, Organisation for Economic
Co-operation and Development

'Macat is taking on some of the major challenges in university education … They have drawn together a strong team of active academics who are producing teaching materials that are novel in the breadth of their approach.'

Prof Lord Broers,
former Vice-Chancellor of the University of Cambridge

'The Macat vision is exceptionally exciting. It focuses upon new modes of learning which analyse and explain seminal texts which have profoundly influenced world thinking and so social and economic development. It promotes the kind of critical thinking which is essential for any society and economy. This is the learning of the future.'

Rt Hon Charles Clarke, former UK Secretary of State for Education

'The Macat analyses provide immediate access to the critical conversation surrounding the books that have shaped their respective discipline, which will make them an invaluable resource to all of those, students and teachers, working in the field.'

Professor William Tronzo, University of California at San Diego

WAYS IN TO THE TEXT

KEY POINTS

- Edward Said was one of the most important cultural figures of the late twentieth century and perhaps the key founder of postcolonial studies.*
- *Orientalism* puts forward the idea that colonialism* is a way to dominate a country, both politically and economically. The book exposes the kind of thinking that helped colonialism take root.
- By reading Said's text, students will acquire an essential framework that will help them to understand both colonialism and postcolonial studies.

Who Was Edward Said?

Edward Said (1935–2003) was one of the most important cultural critics of the late twentieth century. A Palestinian–American academic and political activist, he pioneered the study of how empires*— groups of countries ruled over by one state—developed and functioned. Said's work was so important that he is widely considered to have founded the area of study called postcolonial theory. This field tries to understand how and why colonized countries developed the way they did in a postcolonial era.

Edward Said was born in 1935 in the British Mandate* of

Palestine to a Palestinian mother and a Palestinian–American father. He grew up in Jerusalem and then Cairo, where the family headed in the aftermath of the 1948 Arab–Israeli War.* Said was educated mainly at top British and American schools, but things did not go smoothly. After being expelled from Egypt's Victoria College in 1951, he was sent to an elite boarding school in Massachusetts in the United States. Despite being unhappy there, Said's intelligence shone through and he moved on to study at prestigious Princeton University before gaining his PhD in English Literature at Harvard University in 1964. By this time he was already starting out on an academic career at Columbia University in the department of English and Comparative Literature.

Said's Middle Eastern* background and status as an exile set him apart from his colleagues. Western universities at the time were not multicultural, and Said stood out for being both Arab and foreign. His elite US private education meant, however, that he was both an outsider *and* an insider, which gave him a different intellectual perspective from his colleagues. While he clearly had a great respect for the books he studied—even when he was criticizing them—Said was able to look at Western literature and its links to imperial,* political, and economic realities with a different eye.

Said spent his entire career at Columbia, from 1963 until his death in 2003. His main achievement was in promoting and establishing colonialism as an area of study in the humanities. Published in 1978, *Orientalism* explored the impact of colonialism and Western perceptions of countries that had been colonized. Said explored similar themes in later books, such as *Culture and Imperialism* and *Covering Islam.*

Edward Said became professor of English and comparative literature in 1991, and played a huge part in shaping postcolonial scholarship at Columbia. The university is still home today to a large number of postcolonialist academics.

What Does *Orientalism* Say?

Orientalism is a critique (analysis) of modern European colonialism. The book argues that colonialism was not only a system of political rule, but also an all-round worldview that simply believed the West was superior to the East.

Said examined scholarly debates about Near Eastern* cultures, especially those that were mainly Muslim. He then challenged common Western assumptions about these colonized societies. Because he was looking at academic debates, Said's work in *Orientalism* was designed to show that the academic world was closely connected to the system of political power. Said was seeking to prove that academics had, in effect, collaborated in the West's domination of the East.

Said argued that European colonialism was really about taking advantage of colonized peoples' labor and their resources, while claiming that the Western colonial power was a "savior" helping these societies to be more "modern" like Europe. This was easier for the colonial power to do because it consistently categorized "the Orient" through the use of degrading stereotypes.

Said wrote that this colonialist thinking did not go away when colonial rule ended in the early twentieth century, but continued in different forms. This was made easier when the United States emerged as a huge global power and, according to Said, showed a clearly "Orientalist" view of the world.

Said wanted academics—and society—to admit that racist, colonialist ideas had been supported by Western academic thinking and that the one depended on the other. His ideas were controversial, but there is no doubt that these ideas have helped to change the way colonialism is understood now.

Why Does *Orientalism* Matter?

Orientalism is a very important book that has had a wide influence, both in universities and in politics. It is a key text in postcolonial studies and was considered revolutionary when it first appeared in 1978. Said shows how academic writing can be deeply connected to the politics and workings of colonialism, and how the one fed the other in order to justify the West's self-imposed status as a superior culture. According to Said, colonialism wasn't just the act of colonizing a particular place, it was an all-encompassing way of understanding the world.

Orientalism laid out its arguments in an interdisciplinary* way, breaking down boundaries between academic disciplines. In setting out his arguments, Said covered everything from painting and literature to travel and political writing. In this way the book influenced many areas of study across the humanities and social sciences. As well as bringing a brand new perspective to studies of colonialism, Said's book also challenged academics to look at their own ways of working. For these important reasons *Orientalism* is still an extremely relevant book, and continues to influence and direct scholarly work that looks to understand society and culture.

SECTION 1
INFLUENCES

MODULE 1
THE AUTHOR AND THE
HISTORICAL CONTEXT

KEY POINTS

- When *Orientalism* was first published in 1978, Edward Said was one of a very small number of Arab–American scholars working at elite American universities. He was also one of only a handful who had a deep interest in critically studying modern European colonialism.*

- European colonialism had ended in all but a few parts of the world at this time, but its long-term impact was still very obvious.

- *Orientalism* appeared during a period of great tension between the United States and the Arab world. This tension brought many of the West's historic anti-Arab and anti-Muslim feelings to the surface.

Why Read This Text?

Edward Said's *Orientalism* was published in the United States in 1978 and is a core text in the field of postcolonial studies* and critical theory.* It looked at the West's view of the Orient*—particularly Arab and Muslim civilizations—through academic work, literature, and art. It challenged stereotypical Western views of an Eastern world and culture that was considered inferior. It wanted to show how the world of academia in the West had supported these colonial views and in so doing gave the political powers a kind of intellectual backing to push forward with their colonialist strategies.

What was unusual about *Orientalism* when it first appeared was the fact that it was written by someone who was working at the highest

> ❝ My own experiences of these matters are in part what made me write this book ... the life of an Arab Palestinian in the West, particularly in America, is disheartening. The web of racism, cultural stereotypes, political imperialism,* [and] dehumanizing ideology holding in the Arab or the Muslim is very strong indeed. ❞
>
> Edward Said, *Orientalism*

level of US academia. Other notable anti-colonial* books, such as Frantz Fanon's* *The Wretched of the Earth* (1961)[1] and Aimé Césaire's* *Discourse on Colonialism* (1955),[2] were different, because they were written by authors who were actually living under colonial rule.

Orientalism was published at a time of great social and political change. By the late 1970s, the European imperial* powers had mainly left their colonies and these countries had become independent nations. It was very much a postcolonial world. The Vietnam War* had ended in 1975, but some academics were still criticizing the US for a foreign policy they saw as militaristic and aggressive. This foreign policy was sometimes called "neocolonial," because of the way it still attempted to control other lands, but by means other than direct rule.

In 1972, an attack at the Munich Olympics, in which a Palestinian group called Black September* had killed 11 Israeli Olympic athletes, led to some anti-Arab feeling. Then, in 1973, Israel repelled an attack on its territory by Syria and Egypt (the "Yom Kippur War"),* to some extent thanks to military aid from the United States. The Organization of Arab Petroleum Exporting Countries (OAPEC) retaliated by cutting oil supplies to the West, triggering a worldwide economic crisis. Americans were big consumers of Middle Eastern* oil and so anti-Arab feelings in the US rose again, together with a general sense in the US that Arab identity was linked to terrorist activity.

Interestingly, though, awareness of the issue of race was growing in American public life at this time. The civil rights movement* in the 1960s had fought for equal rights for African-Americans, and the end of legal segregation in the South. This had transformed US politics. Ordinary people were therefore asking questions and examining their cultural perceptions.

All these political and social issues affected Said's arguments and the way *Orientalism* was received.

Author's Life

Edward Said was an intellectual with a high public profile. His studies and his politics were intimately linked. *Orientalism's* arguments and sense of addressing issues that were very much "of the moment" were linked to Said's experiences as an Arab living in the United States.

Said was born in the British Mandate* of Palestine in 1935, and spent his childhood in Jerusalem. After the first Arab–Israeli War* in 1948, a large number of Palestinian Arabs were expelled from Israel. Said's family left for Cairo. There, Edward attended, first, the American school and, later, Victoria College, which modeled itself on the elite British public school system. When speaking about his experience at Victoria College, Said emphasises its anglocentric nature above everything else; in particular, how this environment marked linguistic, cultural, and racial lines between students and teachers. Along with a number of other students at the school, Said felt at home in two or more languages, but only English was allowed to be spoken. Said and his friends used their shared language as an act of defiance to what he saw as an unjust imposition of imperial power. He was taught to think like an English schoolboy, yet he was always made to feel like an outsider: a non-European "other" who should know his place.

After finishing school, Said went to study in the United States, obtaining a degree from Princeton University and a doctorate in English literature from Harvard University. Said saw his school experience repeated at American universities, where again he felt like an outsider. He found himself in an environment that was hostile to Arabs, Arab ideas, and Arab nations, and this experience brought about a major change in his thinking. Here, for the first time, he confronted the paradox of his own identity. Because of his educational background, Said was very familiar with the wealthy, white, and male world of elite academia. *Orientalism* emerges out of this world, and attacks it from within. It examines the ways that Western academia interacts with political power to produce a particular world view. Said struggled to maintain multiple identities within this world, so he began speaking as a Palestinian again, but from within the system. In 1963 he joined the English and comparative literature faculty at Columbia University, and he stayed there until his death in 2003.

Said was fluent in Arabic, English, and French, and could read Spanish, German, Italian, and Latin. His academic specialty was in the area of modern European (mostly British) literature and literary theory. However, his exile from his homeland—and the sense of displacement and alienation this caused in him—was at the heart of much of his work. *Orientalism* was written by a man who intimately understood how the West looked at the Orient, and who therefore could see how this distorted what the *actual* life of an "Oriental" was.

Author's Background

Several different branches of philosophy influenced Said's work and led him to the conclusion that written works are always influenced by the history and politics of the time in which they're written. He was particularly influenced by poststructuralist* philosophy, which described how systems of thought and social organization are built and put into place. The French philosopher Michel Foucault* discusses concepts of power and discourse—the system of thoughts that develop out of verbal interactions and then define how we understand the world—in two important works, *Discipline and Punish*[3] and *The Archaeology of Knowledge*.[4] Foucault particularly looked at how power is underpinned by regulating what can be said, how it can be said, and who can say it. Foucault's work was crucial in forming Said's thinking when he wrote *Orientalism*.

Said wrote: "Texts can *create* not only knowledge, but also the very reality they appear to describe. In time, such knowledge and reality produce a tradition, or what Michel Foucault calls a discourse ..."[5] Said suggested that our modern thinking about the Orient* was created by a power imbalance between Western Europe and the East that existed in the eighteenth and nineteenth centuries.

Orientalism says that European political power, and its academic discourses, in fact produced a concept called the "Orient," which is based on rigid stereotypes and not on the actual cultures of the East. In Said's words: "Orientalism overrode the Orient* ... an observation about a tenth-century Arab poet multiplied itself into a policy towards (and about) the Oriental mentality in Egypt, Iraq, or Arabia ... Orientalism assumed an unchanging Orient, absolutely different from the West ... [It] could never revise itself."[6]

Said was also influenced by the work of Italian Marxist* and political theorist Antonio Gramsci.* Gramsci developed a concept of hegemony,* how one group can come to dominate another. Gramsci looked at how Europe became industrialized in the late nineteenth century and came to the conclusion that the bourgeois,* capitalist* classes grabbed and held on to power not only through force, but also through systems that made sure the working classes—the proletariat*—somehow allowed themselves to be dominated. The bourgeoisie deliberately put forward a worldview that suited them with the express intention of making that view become "normal." When that view came to dominate, it meant that all classes in society came to understand themselves from a bourgeois point of view. This made it seem natural, as well as right, that the elite class dominated everyone else, both economically and politically.

In *Orientalism*, Said applies this same idea to colonial society, saying that even after the imperial powers have left and have granted their colonies independence, the colonialist intellectual standpoint and the dominance of one group over another still remains.

NOTES

1   Frantz Fanon, *The Wretched of the Earth*, trans. Constance Farrington (London: MacGibbon & Kee, 1965).

2   Aimé Césaire, *Discourse on Colonialism*, trans. Joan Pinkham (London & New York: Monthly Review Press, 1972).

3   Michel Foucault, *Discipline and Punish: The Birth of the Prison,* trans. Alan Sheridan (New York: Vintage Books, 1975).

4   Michel Foucault, *The Archaeology of Knowledge*, trans. A. M. Sheridan Smith (London: Tavistock Publications, 1972).

5   Edward Said, *Orientalism* (New York: Vintage Books, 1978), 94.

6   Said, *Orientalism*, 96.

MODULE 2
ACADEMIC CONTEXT

KEY POINTS

- *Orientalism* was crucial in helping found the field of postcolonial studies,* the critical examination of the ways nineteenth- and twentieth-century European colonialism* shaped social, cultural, economic, and political structures on a global level.

- At the time of *Orientalism's* publication, many scholars had written about the negative effects of European colonialism. But no previous scholar had deeply analyzed where the thinking behind colonialism had come from, how it had been nurtured, or how that thinking was still having an influence.

- *Orientalism* drew on pre-existing critical theory* and anti-colonial* thought to create a powerful analysis and critique of European colonialism both as an ideology and as a real system.

The Work in its Context

Edward Said's *Orientalism* brought together two strands of thought: anti-colonialism and critical theory. Anti-colonialism was typified by the thoughts and works of Aimé Césaire* and Frantz Fanon,* who both wrote from inside the colonized culture. It focused on the political gap between the colonizer and the colonized. Critical theory in the social sciences was at that time looking to move away from simply descriptive analyses of systems. Scholars working in this area wanted to develop approaches that would actually change the social arrangements and belief systems that existed. Michel Foucault's* ideas about "discourses,"* or systems of knowledge and meaning, were an

> ❝ No person academically involved with the Near East*—no Orientalist, that is—has ever in the United States culturally and politically identified himself wholeheartedly with the Arabs; certainly there have been identifications on some level, but ... all too frequently they have been radically flawed by their association with discredited political and economic interests (oil-company and State Department Arabists, for example) or with religion. ❞
>
> Edward Said, *Orientalism*

example of this. *Orientalism* drew on both these strands to form a critique of colonialism that showed it to be both a system of rule and a system of ideas.

Said set out to analyze European "Orientalist" work, both scholarly and artistic. He showed how European Orientalist production was in fact a whole system of knowledge. In other words, it could be seen as one of Michel Foucault's "discourses." These discourses don't just provide information about a given subject, they also create the thing they describe. So the Orientalist discourse both described "the East" and created it. No Western representation or discussion of the East could be free from the influence of colonial domination.

Overview of the Field

Orientalism was a product of early twentieth-century anti-colonialism. This anti-colonial feeling was closely related to nationalist independence movements that wanted to end European colonial rule and allow countries to govern themselves. Frantz Fanon, Albert Memmi* and Aimé Césaire all wrote their books while under European imperial* rule and explored the "on the ground" relationship between the colonizer and the colonized. They described the psychological and political damage that colonialism did to everyone involved.

Edward Said was the first person to analyze European cultural history from an "outsider" perspective. He wrote as a colonial, but he was inside the Western Establishment. He used poststructuralist* ideas for his analysis, basing his thinking on the notion that all knowledge is created through different discourses and as such is unstable and changing all the time. Approaching the subject of colonialism in this way made Said one of the most important founders of postcolonial studies.

Postcolonial studies are interdisciplinary* by nature, looking for answers in all of the humanities and social sciences. Its scholars use linguistics,* critical theory, cultural studies, history, and philosophy to analyze how colonialism shaped colonized peoples as well as shaping the Europeans who colonized them. Postcolonial studies focusing on the Middle East* have looked at nineteenth-century books, articles, and pamphlets written about the region to see how they reflect the grand colonial project, that of ruling other regions. Seeing how characters in novels behave or how Middle Eastern people are described in travel guides shows how Europeans viewed "Orientals." This type of analysis is known as discourse analysis, and the process of explaining how texts can reveal ideological standpoints comes from the process of deconstruction,* which was developed by French philosopher Jacques Derrida.*

Said's view was that Western studies of the East were tied to colonial rule itself and actually created colonialism. This was a new way of looking at the subject. After World War II* area studies* became popular. This strand of study focused on knowledge of the politics, literature, economy, and culture of specific areas, such as Middle Eastern Studies. Said saw this way of studying as a direct descendant of colonial-era study and so was naturally dogged by the same type of thinking. The world might have changed politically but, according to

Said, scholars still had a colonial mindset.

When writing *Orientalism,* Said was also influenced by the critical theory of the Frankfurt School.* This group studied the ways that capitalist* thinking was consistently reinforced in popular culture, such as film, music, television, and even horoscopes. The Frankfurt School believed that investigating culture in this way could reveal the hidden workings of capitalist society.

Said didn't entirely follow the Frankfurt School thinking, however. Instead of unmasking and revealing the ways in which dominant forces can subtly use books and music to control, *Orientalism* looked at how literary texts and cultural knowledge actually *are* the power in and of themselves. Because it exposes the system of thought, *Orientalism* is more influenced by Michel Foucault.

Academic Influences

Western universities in the 1970s were mainly dominated by upper-middle-class white men.[1] In Middle Eastern and Islamic studies, this meant that "the scholar" came from a very different background to "the studied." According to Said, this turned "the studied" into an *object* that was looked at and analyzed, rather than individual people who were perfectly capable of expressing themselves to others.

Some writers from colonized countries, and a few Western thinkers like Jean-Paul Sartre,* had written about anti-colonialism by this time. But colonialism as a *system* was still not seriously studied in the humanities. Disciplines such as English literature, philosophy, and history each had strictly defined methods for study.

However, social scientists working in areas such as economics, political science, and sociology were beginning to study both colonialism *and* the political and economic effects of its collapse. Scholars such as the sociologist Immanuel Wallerstein* were starting to question theories of the 1950s and 1960s that stated economic progress would happen everywhere in the world based on how things had evolved when Europe and America were first industrialized. The development of a more complicated world with a global network of different countries relying on each other for all sorts of different things suggested that modernizing wouldn't in fact be so straightforward. Wallerstein talked, for example, about a world systems theory,* where labor throughout the world would not be divided equally and where some states would have all the skilled workers and others the more manual low-paid workers.

It was in this climate that Said decided to look at European art, literature, travel writing, and political writing by colonialist leaders in its entirety. He also studied traditional Orientalist scholarly texts by the likes of Louis Massignon,* Ernest Renan,* and Silvestre de Sacy* to fully explore colonialism and to draw conclusions about it. *Orientalism* boldly ignored boundaries and as such was a genuinely interdisciplinary and innovative work.

NOTES

1   Said discusses the general character of American academia at this time through key examples in his section on the latest phase of Orientalism. See "Orientalism Now" in Said, *Orientalism* (New York: Vintage Books, 1978), 285.

MODULE 3
THE PROBLEM

KEY POINTS

- The central questions that *Orientalism* addresses are: How did the ideology and system of ideas that is the West's study of the East—what can be termed "Orientalism"—begin? And how has it continued to the present day?

- *Orientalism* also asks how the Orientalist system of ideas translated into a concrete, sustained political project.

- Edward Said largely created both the academic and the popular debate about the origins, evolution, and long-term effects of colonialism* as both a means of political rule and as a system of thought.

Core Question

Edward Said's main concern is to explore the relationship between what the West wrote as a description and an explanation of the East and what effect these writings had on colonial power in these territories. It is a book that examined how the way the West *described* the East led to the East actually becoming subservient.

The book addresses this idea by examining cultural texts from both the period of colonial expansion and afterwards. As well as looking at colonialism, the book analyzes how colonialist ideas are still at work in contemporary global affairs.

Scholars were already studying colonialism when Said set out to write *Orientalism*. But these were mainly sociologists and economists who were concerned with investigating the postcolonial* economic system and why there was financial inequality between the West and the formerly colonized territories. Said was more interested in

> ❝ [Orientalism was ultimately a political vision
> of reality whose structure promoted the difference
> between the familiar (Europe, the West, 'us') and the
> strange (the Orient, the East, 'them'). This vision in
> a sense created and then served the two worlds thus
> conceived ... The vision and material reality propped
> each other up, kept each other going. ❞
>
> Edward Said, *Orientalism*

investigating how Western ideas and culture had created colonialism
in the first place. In a review of *Orientalism*, the anthropologist Talal
Asad* wrote that the book was an outstanding work because it tried
to analyze "the *authoritative structure* of Orientalist discourse—the
closed, self-evident, self-confirming character of that distinctive
discourse which is reproduced again and again."[1] In other words,
Western writings displayed an unshakable belief that it understood
this world completely and that all the conclusions it drew about the
East were plainly correct. Said was of the view that although
colonialism was to all intents and purposes dead, this attitude was still
very much alive.

The Participants

Said addressed a number of issues in *Orientalism*. That meant he
contributed to debates in different disciplines, and each debate had
different people taking part. Said looked at how certain fixed ideas—
and the way in which those ideas were expressed in Western culture—
helped shape the West's ongoing views of the East. This thinking had
links to the work of the French philosophers Jacques Derrida* and
Michel Foucault* on language and ideas. Derrida suggested that what
scholars and politicians *said* about topics such as the Middle East*
both summed up their own view and influenced the views of others.[2]

Foucault said that ideas expressed by scholars in discourses* set a boundary beyond which others then could not go.[3] In other words, both Derrida and Foucault thought that discourse controlled the way we see the world. Said took up this idea. He sought to show how scholarly study of the East could first be affected by colonial ideologies and would then in turn reproduce those ideologies.

Said drew on earlier anti-imperial* writing from colonies that had been decolonized,* mainly by the French and the British, in the 1950s and 1960s. Frantz Fanon,* a psychiatrist and writer from Martinique, suggested in his books *Black Skins, White Masks* and *The Wretched of the Earth*[4] that European colonialism had done great psychological damage to the people who had been colonized. Fanon believed that because of their experiences these people had themselves started to believe deep down that they actually *were* racially inferior. Fanon suggested that the language and discourse of colonialism was powerful enough to control not only political systems, but the way individuals felt as well.

In *The Colonizer and the Colonized*,[5] Tunisian writer Albert Memmi* drew on his own experiences as a Tunisian Jew in the French-controlled country. He examined the alienated role of the "privileged minority"—natives who choose to deal with the colonial government. Aimé Césaire's* *Discourse on Colonialism*[6] was a subtle explanation of how colonialism works as a system of domination. The Négritude* literary movement (black French-speaking thinkers who rejected French colonialism) that Césaire helped found built on the work of anti-colonial* writers from Africa and the Middle East to South Asia.

Said was aware of others who had studied the history of Orientalist thought. The French–Egyptian political thinker Anouar Abdel-Malek* wrote as a Marxist,* saying that Europe's economic need for colonies formed the ways Europeans viewed the Middle East. Another Marxist historian, Maxime Rodinson,* showed how the way Europe interacted with the colonies was narrow and dated.[7] And both the Palestinian historian A. L. Tibawi* and the English medievalist R. W. Southern* had written histories of European ideas about the Middle East, its people, and its history.[8]

Said, however, wanted his voice to be heard outside purely scholarly debates. So *Orientalism* was published by a commercial publisher. Said was keen for his view on Orientalism to be heard by everyone at a time when the conflicts in the Middle East of the early 1970s were still fresh in people's memories. While *Orientalism* was responding to scholars, it was also a work that was rooted in the real world of the time.

The Contemporary Debate

Said's willingness to make major criticisms in his work set him apart from other scholars, but he still acknowledged the importance of earlier writers to what he was doing. Indeed, he dedicated *Orientalism* to Ibrahim Abu-Lughod,* who had reshaped the story of Arab history by showing how European ideas translated into Arab culture and how Arab cultures then changed or rejected these ideas as part of their own cultural development. Abu-Lughod wrote "counter-hegemonic"* analyses of Middle East history. Those histories rejected the idea that colonies were completely passive under imperial* power and simply accepted their rule. If Arab cultures changed and rejected European ideas, he pointed out, then the Arab colonies could not be passive in the way Europeans had always thought they were. But Said went further than Abu-Lughod, by looking at how the transformation of European ideas affected the European colonialists themselves.

The Pakistani political scientist and writer Eqbal Ahmad* also questioned Orientalism, but he looked at it in terms of economic power. Ahmad investigated the way in which countries like France and Britain misused their colonialist power to profit from their colonies economically. They created economic growth in their own lands by abusing colonized people as a cheap workforce operating in very poor conditions and by taking natural resources for themselves.[9] In contrast to Ahmad, Said saw Orientalism more as a set of ideas that came about because of political views. He did not focus on the economic questions Ahmad examined. But he didn't dismiss them either. Said's investigation of Orientalism went across a range of different concerns, which made *Orientalism* a more complete examination of the issues than anything that had come before.

NOTES

1   Talal Asad, "Review: *Orientalism* by Edward Said," *The English Historical Review* 95.376 (July 1980), 648–9.

2   Jacques Derrida, *Writing and Difference*, trans. Alan Bass (Chicago: Chicago University Press, 1978).

3   Michael Foucault, *The Archaeology of Knowledge*, trans. A. M. Sheridan Smith (London: Tavistock Publications, 1972).

4   Frantz Fanon, *The Wretched of the Earth*, trans. Constance Farrington (London: MacGibbon & Kee, 1965)

5   Albert Memmi, *The Colonizer and the Colonized* (London: The Orion Press, 1965).

6   Aimé Césaire, *Discourse on Colonialism*, trans. Joan Pinkham (London & New York: Monthly Review Press, 1972).

7   A. L. Tibawi, "Revue des études mohammediennes," *Revue historique* 461 (1969): 169–220.

8   A. L. Tibawi, "English-speaking Orientalists: A Critique of Their Approach to Islam and Arab Nationalism," *Islamic Quarterly* 8 (1964): 25–45; R. W. Southern, *Western Views of Islam in the Middle Ages* (Cambridge: Harvard University Press, 1962).

9   Carollee Bengelsdorf, Margaret Cerullo, and Yogesh Chandrani, eds., *The Selected Writings of Eqbal Ahmad*, (New York: Columbia University Press, 2006).

MODULE 4
THE AUTHOR'S CONTRIBUTION

KEY POINTS

- Said was influenced by anti-colonial* thinking about colonialism's* impact and also by contemporary critical theory* that looked at modern systems of thought. This helped him put together a revolutionary argument about the past, present, and future effects of colonialism worldwide.

- Said said that the end of colonial rule did not put an end to colonial ways of thinking. In fact, this type of thinking was still evident in many humanities disciplines, such as Middle East* studies.

- Said's belief that Western academic work had been extremely important in developing the West's entire Orientalist worldview made some of his fellow academics defensive, while others took another look at what they had been doing.

Author's Aims

Edward Said's *Orientalism* changed its field. It merged critical theory and intellectual history (the way major ideas have developed historically) to trace how the Western imagination developed its ideas about the Orient. Said wanted to outline both how scholars had built up this idea of the East, and how the idea had developed over time. He wanted to show how these views had been deeply linked to the expansion of European colonial power across the world. He did this by combining literary criticism and analysis to understand how Orientalist discourse* became a "carrier" of colonialist ideas and attitudes. So the book deliberately politicized the way we look at

> **❝** [*Orientalism's*] outstanding contribution lies in
> its attempt to analyze the authoritative structure of
> Orientalist discourse—the closed, self-evident, self-
> confirming character of that distinctive discourse which
> is reproduced again and again. **❞**
>
> Talal Asad,* "Review: *Orientalism* by Edward Said," *English Historical Review*

literary and artistic work in this area. This is Said's key academic
innovation. Debates in postcolonial* and cultural studies will now
often start with a look at how things are represented in texts, in images,
and in sound.

Said also set his work apart by providing evidence from lots of
different text sources, from scholarly works in history and anthropology
right through to novels and poetry.

Orientalism is at its heart a history of how cultures represent
things, in this case how Europe depicts the East. *Orientalism* describes
the Western view of the Orient* as "ignorant but complex." According
to Said, this construction of a view of the East exists and reinforces
itself according to its own internal logic.[1] The section of the book
called "Orientalism Now" describes the Orient that appears as "a
system of representations framed by a whole set of forces that brought
the Orient into Western learning, Western consciousness, and later,
Western empire.*"[2]

Orientalism's main aim was to investigate how this "system of
representations" combines to create a vision where a strange,
unchanging, and inferior "Orient" is compared to a modern and
superior "Occident"* (the West).

Approach

Said's argument has three parts. His first theme is "The Scope of
Orientalism." This section of the book looks at the boundaries of

Orientalist representation through geography and across time. His second theme is "Orientalist Structures and Restructures." Here Said looks at the images, the interests, and the institutions that Orientalist scholarship helped to shape. The third section of Said's book, "Orientalism Now," analyzes the shift in Orientalist thinking that happened after World War I.*

Said's argument is mainly theoretical. He wasn't looking to make specific factual claims, but wanted to explain the ways in which the West's image of the East had been created. He wanted to show the various combining elements that made this view possible and encouraged it to flourish.

Said brought together theories and ideas from many writers and academic disciplines, and was inspired by philosophers like the Frenchmen Michel Foucault* and Jacques Derrida.* Their ideas about how to analyze discourse formed the basis of Said's own approach and allowed him to show how representations of the Orient were full of implied meanings.

Contribution in Context

Orientalism is an analysis that investigates many different areas in order to understand how politics—and colonialism in particular—influences works of culture and scholarship that are supposedly "objective" and "pure."

Said saw the way the Orient* is perceived as an imaginary view that had been constructed by Western Europe so that it could justify and then impose economic and political control of other lands. This was a new idea, at least on the systematic and cross-regional scale that Said suggested it happened.

Said was not particularly interested in pointing out individual instances of stereotyping or generalizing. Rather, he studied the ways in which those instances had evolved and helped colonizers to take political, economic, and social control. This was radically different from how "Oriental" societies had been studied up till then with Western scholarship's focus on "area studies." Those "areas"—the Middle East and South, Central, and Southeast Asia—were terms, Said argued, that grew from a colonial vision.

Said suggested that the terms themselves were closely tied to Cold War* American political interests, and he discusses this relationship at length in his book's closing chapter, "Orientalism Now: The Latest Phase."[3] In "explaining" those politically important areas for what was assumed to be a Western audience, area studies often used familiar Orientalist stereotypes. So it was common for Islam to be portrayed as somehow backward and not interested in progress, and for Oriental societies to be described as unchanging and mysterious to the West.

Because *Orientalism* was Said's first major academic publication, it can be seen as the important first step in the author's career as a high-profile public intellectual. Said would return to the ideas he put forward in *Orientalism* later in his career. His book *Culture and Imperialism* applied his theories on colonialism to European cultural works, examining the way in which colonialism was openly explained in the Western world, as well as the way that ideas on Orientalism were implied. Whereas *Orientalism* primarily dealt with Orientalist scholarly works, *Culture and Imperialism* looked at how Orientalist ways of thinking appeared in great European literary works by writers such as Jane Austen,* William Butler Yeats,* and Joseph Conrad.*

Said's later political and academic work about Palestinian identity and independence also drew on the ideas in *Orientalism,* looking at the ways in which racist, colonial portrayals of Arab ethnicity still influenced modern Western treatment of the Palestinians.

NOTES

1   Edward Said, *Orientalism* (New York: Vintage Books, 1978), 55.

2   Said, *Orientalism*, 202–3.

3   Said, *Orientalism*, 284–328.

SECTION 2
IDEAS

MODULE 5
MAIN IDEAS

KEY POINTS

- Said argues that Orientalism is a system of thought that casts the West as superior and the East as inferior, and so justifies the West's domination of the East.

- *Orientalism* says that the Western view of the East is a fantasy of a world that is unchanging and exotic, and one that bears little resemblance to the complex reality.

- Because this is a subject that was very personal to him as an Arab and as an intellectual working in the university system, Said makes his arguments openly and forcefully, setting out his ideas clearly at the beginning of the book and then developing those ideas consistently throughout.

Key Themes

Edward Said's central concerns in *Orientalism* are power, how people and countries are represented in cultural and academic work, and how Western European thinking actually helped create the Orient* as it was. For Said, the term "Orient" does not refer to a concrete place or culture, but to an intellectual idea, an invented concept of a way of life that was created to be the total opposite of European civilization. Once this idea had been constructed, European colonial powers could then define themselves in direct contrast to their colonies—as rational rather than emotional and as civilized rather than barbaric. Said writes that Western academics played an important part in the creation of this Oriental stereotype, and that they helped to create a "Western style for dominating, restructuring, and having authority over the Orient." "European culture," he added, "gained in strength and identity by

> 66 My thesis is that the essential aspects of modern Orientalist theory and praxis (from which present-day Orientalism derives) can be understood, not as a sudden access of objective knowledge about the Orient,* but as a set of structures inherited from the past, secularized,* redisposed, and re-formed by such disciplines as philology, which in turn were naturalized [and] modernized. 99
>
> Edward Said, *Orientalism*

setting itself off against the Orient* as a sort of surrogate and even underground self."[1]

Said sets out his thesis in terms of:

- textuality* (the characteristic of a text that communicates meaning)
- geographic-temporal imagination* (the idea that a place or a type of people can exist not only in reality, but as a made-up idea that is based around shared geography and history and is then built on with stories)
- the clear links between Orientalist scholarship and Western domination.

His argument operates on two levels: one examines Orientalist cultural works with an emphasis on content; the other explains the political dynamics that made Orientalism possible. The Palestinian–American anthropologist Nadia Abu El Haj* suggests that "*Orientalism* sought not just to map out a particular discursive formation* but, just as crucially, to elaborate on how that discursive formation articulated with state power—its institutions, its economic and military imperial* projects."[2]

In effect, *Orientalism* was written to show that Western Oriental studies did not analyze the East in an objective fashion, but instead "created" an East that, in fact, *deserved* to be under imperial control.

Exploring the Ideas

Orientalism moves across time and across academic disciplines, but the book remains tightly organized around a central set of problems. Said uses an extended Introduction to outline the text's central aims: to examine the intellectual development of Orientalism both as a discipline and as a category, and to show the ways in which it helped create the colonial project. In the chapter, "Imaginative Geography and its Representations: Orientalizing the Oriental," Said describes the fantasy of the Orient that scholars developed. Geography, in the Orientalist imagination, becomes linked to a place in time. The Orient appears to "alternate in the mind's geography between being an Old World to which one returned, as to Eden or Paradise … and being a wholly new place to which one came … in order to set up a New World."[3]

What Said is suggesting is that the East represents a "less evolved" stage of civilization—so much so that it appears to exist in a wholly different world and time. This is a common view and can be seen when romantic descriptions of the East describe it as the source of the mystical or religious roots of civilization. All this, Said argues, was useful in helping the West justify European colonialism.* It made it possible for the West to claim that its presence was needed so that the East could reform, rebuild, and somehow find itself again. This view, of course, assumed that the ability to make such changes was something the Oriental himself was not equipped to do.

As a second major theme, Said emphasizes the difference between what he called "latent" Orientalism and "manifest" Orientalism. This is an important aspect of his thinking.

"Latent" Orientalism, in Said's view, is the beliefs and assumptions that underpin Western Orientalist study. The most important of these is the belief that the West is quite simply superior to the East: more civilized and more rational. This view was born out of Western study and then spread outwards to lay the groundwork for, and then actually enable, colonial rule. This view of Western superiority justified an ongoing Western presence—both scholarly and political—in the Orient. By saying that the civilization of the West was superior to that of the East, it allowed the West to justify the idea that the East should be "studied" and that the West could intervene in the East whenever it saw fit. This meant that the East becomes a place that has things done to it, rather than doing things itself. Static and without its own history, this Orient is at best just a container for the glories of ancient civilizations. And these civilizations somehow need the West to help reestablish them.

"Manifest" Orientalism, on the other hand, is a physical, institutional presence: it can be found in university departments, cultural works, and the structures of government behind colonial rule.

Put together, these two forms of Orientalism define a discourse,* an exchange of thoughts and ideas between East and West. However, it is manifest Orientalism—and the connections between the latent and the manifest—that forms the core of Said's argument. He sets out the idea that while latent Orientalism does not change very much over time, the concrete examples of manifest Orientalism in action do change according to political and economic circumstances:[4]

"The distinction I am making is really between an almost unconscious (and certainly untouchable) positivity, which I shall call *latent* Orientalism, and the various stated views about Oriental society, languages, literatures, history, sociology, and so forth, which I shall call *manifest* Orientalism. Whatever change occurs in knowledge of the Orient is found almost exclusively in manifest Orientalism; the unanimity, stability, and durability of latent Orientalism are more or less constant."[5]

Said's third theme discusses how the West comes to know the East.

He sees Orientalism from the eighteenth century onwards as part of a more general cultural shift towards secular and scientific rationalism, i.e. a world less concerned with religious matters and based more on reason. From this viewpoint the world is a place of chaos, a place that needs to be brought under control and categorized. He writes that "the specific intellectual and institutional structures of modern Orientalism" rely on four currents of thought in eighteenth-century culture:"expansion, historical confrontation, sympathy, classification."[6] Said suggested that scholars of the time had therefore decided that the Orient was a place that needed to be tamed, understood, and eventually brought back to good health through "scientific" study and the "help" of the West.

It is here that Said gives evidence of Orientalist scholarship justifying the need for empire* ahead of actual colonization. For Said, Western knowledge about the Orient is information that is gathered and organized specifically in order to gain future political and economic control over that region. Similarly, the Western desire to classify everything Oriental "properly" leaves no room for things to vary, change, or develop; the Orient becomes nothing more than a passive, static object that can be investigated, shaped, and then acted on. In short, it becomes an object that can be colonized.

Language and Expression

Orientalism is a powerful book, not least because Said is so personally involved with its subject matter. The political urgency in his writing flows from his own experiences in the British colonies and the United States. "Much of the personal investment in this study derives from my awareness of being an 'Oriental' as a child growing up in two British colonies," he writes. "The web of racism, cultural stereotypes, political imperialism, dehumanizing ideology holding in the Arab or the Muslim is very strong indeed … The nexus of knowledge and power creating 'the Oriental' and in a sense obliterating him as a human being is therefore not for me an exclusively academic matter."[7]

Said looks to show that the Orientalist academic is defined by a deep sense of detachment and "otherness." His job is to dispassionately interpret "alien" cultures to a European audience. In contrast, Said was open and unapologetic about his own experience and identity, and how this affected his academic work. This attitude clearly challenged the notion of "objectivity" that was believed to be essential in order for scholars to be seen as credible in the Western world of academia, and, according to Said, even more so in the field of Orientalism.

Said's argument is generally set out in a clear, eloquent, and forceful manner. He does use some conceptual and academic language that may be hard to understand at first, but this is a deliberate tactic. His aim in publishing the book was to produce a strong critique of colonialism (and to imply the systemic racism that lay behind it), for a Western academic audience. This audience was often hostile to such ideas. Said used academic language as a way of speaking directly to this audience. But he also wrote in a way that interested readers could generally understand, meaning that the book became popular both in academic circles and with a much wider audience.

NOTES

1   Edward Said, *Orientalism* (New York: Vintage Books, 1978), 3.

2   Nadia Abu El Haj, "Edward Said and the Political Present," *American Ethnologist* 32, no. 4 (November 2004), 548.

3   Said, *Orientalism*, 58.

4   Said, *Orientalism*, 222–4.

5   Said, *Orientalism*, 206.

6   Said, *Orientalism*, 120.

7   Said, *Orientalism*, 27.

MODULE 6
SECONDARY IDEAS

KEY POINTS

- Edward Said's primary ideas lay out his big thinking about Orientalism and the political, economic, and social conditions that brought it about. His secondary ideas detail the particular stereotypes attached to the Orient in the Orientalist's view.

- The stereotypes of Orientalism that Said identifies include: seeing the Oriental as fundamentally alien and "Other;" viewing the Orient as representing aspects of European society (particularly emerging aspects born out of industrialization) that upper-class Europeans feared and wished to reject; and regarding the Orient as "feminine" (meaning weak and in need of help and direction) in the Victorian, European sense.

- Of his secondary ideas, Said's most important concept is that of the Oriental as someone "Other," someone who represents the complete opposite of the West.

Other Ideas

Edward Said's main ideas in *Orientalism* deal with the ways in which the academic disciplines researching the Orient were totally associated with exerting political power in the colonies. His secondary ideas explain how Orientalism showed itself in European cultural productions such as books, articles, and pamphlets. Said identifies the core beliefs about the Orient and Oriental people that underpin Orientalism as a field of study. These core beliefs then underpin the whole colonial* project.

> **"** The very possibility of development, transformation, human movement—in the deepest sense of the word—is denied the Orient* and the Oriental. As a known and ultimately an immobilized or unproductive quality, they come to be identified with a bad sort of eternality. **"**
>
> Edward Said, *Orientalism*

Said pays particular attention to the sub-disciplines that he believes are central to Orientalist discourse,* namely philology—the study of written language, blending history and linguistics*—and anthropology, the study of culture.

Orientalism develops a powerful central argument, but its secondary ideas are skillfully woven into the work's broader scope. These ideas help to flesh out the bigger argument concerning the political power that Orientalism seeks to justify and sustain.

The book also incorporates a structure behind its arguments that is based on the work of French philosopher Michel Foucault.* Foucault's interest was in analyzing discourses—the written information that builds up around how a subject is treated throughout a culture. Discourse analysis is a vital part of Said's approach. Being able to analyze texts using this technique allowed Said to explore the issues in a methodical way and back his ideas up with evidence.

Exploring the Ideas

Said's most important secondary idea was to show how common Orientalist stereotypes always positioned an Oriental as an object and a European as someone who was questioning, interpreting, and somehow rescuing them. In Said's words: "To be a European in the Orient *always* involves being a consciousness set apart from, and unequal with, its surroundings."[1] The Oriental person is portrayed as impenetrable, overly religious, and completely different from the

Westerner. This creates a sense of distance. Said uses the story of the British colonial bureaucrat gone "native" T. E. Lawrence*—also known as "Lawrence of Arabia"—to show that even in this situation the Orient is created as nothing more than a stage where Western male "heroism" can be played out in dramatic fashion.

Stripped of humanity and all its complexity, the Oriental became a blank canvas for any identity a Westerner might choose. The Oriental was seen as somehow naturally backward, against modernity, morally depraved, and likely to do things to excess. Indeed, an Oriental was often compared to and explicitly associated with degenerate people. As Said explains: "The Oriental was linked to elements in Western society (delinquents, the insane, women, the poor) having in common an identity best described as lamentably alien ... Orientals were ... analyzed not as citizens, or even people, but as problems to be solved or confined or ... taken over."[2]

In this view, the Orient can be seen as a projection of European social anxieties at the dawn of a new age—the modern age of industrial capitalism.* This was a time when social structures in the West were undergoing massive changes, and issues such as urban poverty and overpopulation, and the public health crises that came with them, began to emerge. Prompted by the publication of Charles Darwin's *On the Origin of Species* in 1859, ideas about evolution also informed Orientalist thought and placed the East as fundamentally backward in terms of scientific progress and human history.

Said also briefly discusses the strong sexual undertones that are present in this attitude. He identifies the often erotic tone found in the prose of Orientalist writers as a way of associating the Orient with a Victorian viewpoint of femininity. This view saw females— and therefore the Orient itself—as fundamentally weak, incapable of thinking or acting for themselves or itself, seductive by nature, yet passive, and inviting male intervention and penetration.

Said talks about this at great length in his discussion of French novelist Gustave Flaubert's* writings on the Orient. According to Said these writings showed "an almost uniform association between the Orient and sex."[3] The Orient, then, is a kind of male fantasy object, with the Orientalist "hero" being allowed to transform his sexual desire into enlightenment for the Orient. The Orient's supposedly feminine weakness actively invites "benevolent" paternalism* from the white European male.

Overlooked

Orientalism is the foundational text of postcolonial studies* in Western academia. But it has reached far beyond this particular environment and has gone on to become a world classic. Translated into more than 36 languages, it has been fiercely debated, dissected, and expanded on for decades.

As a result, there are no areas of the work that have been clearly neglected. Critics and scholars have examined, discussed, and drawn from many individual aspects of the text. However, Said's original arguments have often been lost in the highly politicized controversy that surrounded the author as a public intellectual. This became a more important factor after Said started to get more involved in the Israeli–Palestine issues* in the late 1980s.

NOTES

1   Edward Said, *Orientalism* (New York: Vintage Books, 1978), 157.

2   Said, *Orientalism*, 207.

3   Said, *Orientalism*, 188.

MODULE 7
ACHIEVEMENT

KEY POINTS

- Edward Said was successful in achieving his aims: *Orientalism* and the debate that followed established colonialism* as a field of serious and active scholarly study.

- *Orientalism* was published at a key moment in world politics: While European colonialism had for the most part ended, it had become very clear by the late 1970s that it had totally shaped the global economic, political, and cultural landscape. In many cases this had not been a good thing.

- *Orientalism's* originality increased its impact in certain ways and limited it in others: Since Said's argument was fairly new, many initial reactions failed to take into account his more subtle and complex ideas.

Assessing the Argument

Orientalism largely succeeded in what it set out to do. It aimed to encourage a debate about colonialism and bring about an era of postcolonial studies.* The book had a methodology and framework for examining imperialism—and afterwards it was used by scholars to produce more investigations into colonial and postcolonial culture.

Said's work provided a worldview and vocabulary that could potentially be used to destabilize white Euro–American supremacy outside the university system. Perhaps more subtly, though, *Orientalism* also inspired a trend towards reflection and internal criticism *within* the disciplines of the humanities and social sciences. The book prompted scholars to look at their own approach to the subject dispassionately. It also made them question what was being produced in academic circles

> ❝ *Orientalism* sought not just to map out a particular discursive* formation but, just as crucially, to elaborate on how that discursive formation articulated with state power—its institutions, its economic and military imperial* projects. ❞
>
> Nadia Abu El Haj,* "Edward Said and the Political Present," *American Ethnologist*

on the subject of formerly colonized peoples and how those works could reinforce old colonial power relationships.

Said argued that there were still very clear examples of the tight relationship between academic scholarship in the West and Western countries still being able to exert political influence over people who had once been colonized. He said this was particularly evident in area studies* scholarship. Said discusses this idea at length in the final section of *Orientalism*.[1] According to him, area studies as a discipline divides the world into regions using colonial categories (for example, the "Middle East"* and "Near East"*), and then produces knowledge that tries to "explain" politically important non-Western societies to Euro-American governments.

People continue to debate and engage with *Orientalism*. It could be said that Said's analysis is more important than ever in the post-9/11* world. Certain Middle Eastern countries where Muslims are in the majority have had Western military forces on the ground. The debate among the general Western population, meanwhile, is certainly colored by the Orientalist worldview.

Achievement in Context

Orientalism appeared in 1978 at an important time in the relationship between the West and the East as conflict was rife. This helped it to reach a wider audience, but also hindered useful interpretations of the book.

University scholars in relevant areas were generally not very interested in ideas of colonialism and how colonized countries were represented and they reacted badly to any suggestion that they might not be objective. Critical analysis of colonialism that did exist tended to focus on economics and social sciences such as sociology, rather than on culture.

Following recent international events there was also a wave of anti-Islamic feeling in the United States and Western Europe. This brought the tension between the West on the one hand and the Arab and Muslim East on the other out into the open. The Iranian Revolution* of 1979 raised these tensions to fever pitch. This volatile political climate meant that *Orientalism* received a lot of attention from both academics and the general public. It sparked fierce debate and some people were quick to condemn the work.

The publication of *Orientalism* also coincided with a growing disillusionment with postcolonial rule. From 1945 to 1970 there had been a sense of real optimism among newly independent former colonies. But the 1980s saw the rise of dictators like Idi Amin* in Uganda and Robert Mugabe* in Zimbabwe. And there was both a widespread economic crisis and growing poverty in many former colonies. These factors led to a re-examination of the process of decolonization* as people questioned what had been gained.

These factors contributed to the widespread attention *Orientalism* received. They also helped to spread Said's ideas throughout the academic world and among the general public. The book was controversial and so became a lightning rod for attracting both praise and criticism, in ways that often failed to take into account the subtleties of Said's arguments.

But because *Orientalism* was talked about so much, it did inspire many people to think about colonialism. The significant postcolonial scholarship the book inspired proves the point.

Limitations

Orientalism is intentionally limited in its scope. It is solely concerned with what was relatively recent European colonialism. So the book is deeply rooted in its geographic and historical context, and concerns itself with a specific epistemology,* or theory of knowledge, and a specific set of historical processes.

Some scholars have questioned Said's dependence on French philosopher Michel Foucault's* concepts of discursive formation* (the type of written, spoken, or performed communication that forms the basis of analysis) and disciplinary power* (the way a dominant group exerts its authority over a dominated group) in analyzing materials.

The attention Said gave to a few Orientalist thinkers doesn't truly fit in with Foucault's firm ideas about discourse* analysis. Foucault saw power as absolute, and believed it would work its way into *all* knowledge. This meant that Foucault thought that discourses could not be avoided or changed by any one writer. To Foucault, the individual is totally irrelevant in discourse analysis. Said drew heavily from this concept of discourse, but then he focused on just a few individual authors. His argument was that the writers he looked at were representative of all Orientalist thinkers, and that they did, in fact, change Orientalism as a discipline.

Said himself accepted that this was a problem of sorts. He wrote in an afterword:"*Orientalism* is a partisan book, not a theoretical machine ... The interest I took in Orientalism as a cultural phenomenon ... derives from its variability and unpredictability ... What I tried to preserve in my analysis of Orientalism was its combination of consistency *and* inconsistency, its play, so to speak."[2] Any reader of the text has to accept that there is some intellectual tension between two theoretical notions: humanism* (where humans have the power to affect systems of thought) and Foucault's idea of power.

NOTES

1   Edward Said, *Orientalism* (New York: Vintage Books, 1978), 284–328.

2   Said, *Orientalism*, 339–40.

MODULE 8
PLACE IN THE AUTHOR'S WORK

KEY POINTS

- Said published a great deal of work on colonialism,* postcolonialism,* and contemporary global politics, particularly focusing on the Middle East.* Orientalism is considered his greatest work. It is his most influential book and the one for which he is most famous.

- *Orientalism* contained Said's key ideas and views on colonialism and postcolonialism. These ideas had their roots in his previous work and would continue to be important to him throughout his career.

- *Orientalism* is a very personal book, reflecting Said's own experiences as well as his academic concerns.

Positioning

In his long and varied career, Edward Said concentrated mainly on colonialism and its legacies. He wanted to understand and dismantle racist, colonialist mental frameworks, and explore what he saw as more human alternatives. This was his project from the very beginning of his career.

Said's first book, published in 1966, looked at the Polish–British author Joseph Conrad.* *Joseph Conrad and the Fiction of Autobiography*[1] discussed Conrad's anxieties about his own life and identity and how he wrote about the past in his novels. Said felt there was a clear connection between the two. He uses Conrad as a way to represent a larger crisis of the European sense of self when faced with a modern, industrialized world.

After writing a book called *Beginnings: Intentions and Method* about

> 66 Can one divide human reality, as indeed human reality seems to be divided, into clearly different cultures, histories, traditions, societies, even races, and survive the consequences humanly? By surviving the consequences humanly, I mean to ask whether there is any way of avoiding the hostility expressed by the division, say, of men into 'us' (Westerners) and 'they' (Orientals). 99
>
> Edward Said, *Orientalism*

the intellectual origins of literary theory in 1975,[2] Said published *Orientalism* in 1978. *The Question of Palestine* followed a year later. In 1981, two years after the Iranian Revolution*, came the Iran hostage crisis, where 52 American diplomats and citizens were held hostage by students in the American Embassy in the capital Tehran. In the same year Said published *Covering Islam: How the Media and the Experts Determine How We See the Rest of the World*,[3] in which he argued that contemporary representations of Muslims continued the old colonial discourses about the Orient.

In *Culture and Imperialism,* published in 1993, Said looked at both Western artistic and scholarly production and Euro–American imperialism.* The book contained some of Said's most important examinations of Western literature and empire,* including discussions on Joseph Conrad, Jane Austen,* and William Butler Yeats.*

Freud and the Non-European,[4] published in 2003, built on Said's work on Western psychologies, identity, and modernity as he further investigated political and cultural identity. Here Said connected the Austrian psychologist Sigmund Freud's* important book *Moses and Monotheism*[5] to modern Middle Eastern politics to suggest it might be possible to build political and cultural identity in a different way.

Orientalism aside, Said is perhaps best known for his involvement with Palestine and the Israeli–Palestinian conflict,* not only as a scholar but also as an activist. While he obviously had a personal interest in this issue, Said also saw this conflict as being clearly connected to the bigger issues of European colonialism and how it had affected world politics in general. He wrote four books on the subject of Palestine. The first of these, *The Question of Palestine*[6] is a key text offering a detailed analysis of modern Palestine and the Palestinian people. One of its most important chapters, "Zionism from the Standpoint of its Victims," was even published separately as an article.[7]

In addition, *The Politics of Dispossession: The Struggle for Palestinian Self-Determination, 1969–1994,*[8] details the history of both the Palestinian people (inside and outside Israel) and the Palestinian Territories in the aftermath of the 1967 Six-Day War.* In 1986 Said collaborated with the photographer Jean Mohr * to produce *After the Last Sky*. This book explored in words and images how it felt to be a displaced, exiled Palestinian. Said's most personal autobiographical work—*Out of Place: A Memoir*[9]—appeared in 1999 and describes his own experience of exile growing up as a Palestinian in Jerusalem, then Egypt, and eventually in the United States.

Integration

As Said's academic background was in English literature, most of his work is classed as literary analysis or cultural studies. In his 1966 book *Joseph Conrad and the Fiction of Autobiography*, for example, Said investigates Conrad's novel *Heart of Darkness*. He analyzes how Conrad used the East as a kind of theatre where Europeans could try to play out and understand their own psychological issues. Conrad's Orientals appear as part of the backdrop to his work or as foils, but they are never the principal characters.[10]

Said's work has a wide range and can't be fitted neatly into one category. This can be seen in *Orientalism*, which was an interdisciplinary* book drawing on many different areas of study. Said intended it to break down barriers that limited perception and thought, and hoped that his work could contribute to change Orientalist discourses. As his career progressed, Said became better known for his political writings on Palestine and on popular Western representations of the Middle East. His view that colonialism was a deeply engrained system of thought and a tangible form of domination had a wide impact on people's understanding and views of the Israeli–Palestinian conflict.[11]

Significance

Orientalism had a major impact on all scholarly work that dealt with colonialism. Said's ideas were a direct challenge to his fellow academics and they drew together several strands of thought that had not been fully considered until then. This meant that the book has had a lasting impact on both how the East is studied and how it is understood.

Orientalism is also significant in Said's career and can easily be considered as his master work. It certainly cemented his public reputation as an important scholar of cultural studies. *Orientalism* also helped to inspire critical re-evaluations in the fields of history, anthropology, and literature, while also causing a great deal of controversy. All this makes it reasonable to see *Orientalism* as Edward Said's single most important contribution to the study of colonialism and its aftereffects.

NOTES

1   Edward Said, *Joseph Conrad and the Fiction of Autobiography* (Cambridge: Harvard University Press, 1966).

2   Edward Said, *Beginnings: Intentions and Method* (New York: Columbia University Press, 1985).

3   Edward Said, *Covering Islam: How the Media and the Experts Determine How We See the Rest of the World* (New York: Vintage Books, 1997).

4   Edward Said, *Freud and the non-European* (London: Verso, 2003).

5   Sigmind Freud, *Moses and Monotheism* (London: Hogarth Press, 1939).

6   Edward Said, *The Question of Palestine* (New York: Vintage Books, 1979).

7   Edward Said, "Zionism from the Standpoint of Its Victims," *Social Text* No. 1 (1979), 7–58.

8   Edward Said, *The Politics of Dispossession: The Struggle for Palestinian Self-Determination 1969–1994* (New York: Pantheon Books, 1994).

9   Edward Said, *Out of Place: A Memoir* (New York: Knopf, 1999).

10 Said, *Joseph Conrad*.

11 Said, *Question of Palestine*.

SECTION 3
IMPACT

MODULE 9
THE FIRST RESPONSES

KEY POINTS

- Because it is a highly political work with a clear political viewpoint, each critic's own political views, particularly with regard to issues of race, ethnicity, and colonialism,* shaped their reaction to *Orientalism*.

- Some critics felt that Orientalism was misrepresented in the book, claiming it was not a discipline that was intimately connected to the political project of colonialism.

- Other critics argued that Said failed to take into account the complexities of the colonial relationship.

Criticism

Orientalism ignited a storm of controversy, because it was a work that took direct critical aim at the Western academic world—both historically and in the present day. Critics of the work fell broadly into two groups. The first consisted mostly of academic Orientalists defending their field against Edward Said's criticisms.

The second group was more generally sympathetic to Said's point of view, but critical of his use of theory. Several scholars in both camps analyzed the scope and choice of Said's material, noting the fact that he didn't look at East and South Asia in his work. Nor did he examine German, Dutch, and Russian Orientalist scholarship. Said openly acknowledged these criticisms, but still defended his decision to focus his studies on the Islamic "Near East"* and to British and French scholarship.

They also objected to Said's view of Western studies of Orientalism, saying it was both too rigid and inaccurate. Bernard Lewis,* professor

> 66 What imperial* purpose was served by deciphering
> the ancient Egyptian language, for example, and then
> restoring to the Egyptians knowledge of and pride in
> their forgotten, ancient past? 99
>
> Bernard Lewis, *Islam and the West*

emeritus of Islamic history at Princeton University and one of the
most influential Western scholars of the Middle East,* published a
scathing review of *Orientalism* in the *New York Review of Books*. This led
to a frank exchange of views with Said in the "Letters to the Editor"
section of the magazine. Lewis said that Said was guilty of more than
simple mistakes as a scholar and saw their difference of opinion as
fundamentally based in different ideological views. "Apparently
unwilling to defend his interpretation of Orientalism—a branch of
scholarship—on a scholarly level," he wrote, "Mr. Said insists on
politicizing the whole question and assigning a political significance
not only to his own statements but also to those of any who have the
temerity to question his facts and methods."[1]

Lewis especially objected to Said's link between Orientalism as an
area of study and Europe's empire*-building policies. He felt this view
made the arguments too simplistic and that it was unfair to Orientalism
as a discipline. Lewis said that Orientalism's wide range of interests
showed how limited Said's argument was.[2] Other critics pointed out
that Europeans had been studying the Islamic world since long before
the modern age of empire.

Some academics, meanwhile, have simply ignored Said's
arguments. In his book *The Clash of Civilizations and the Remaking of
World Order*, published in 1996, the American political scientist Samuel
Huntington,* argued that future global conflicts would develop out
of cultural differences and that Islam was directly opposed to "Western
civilization."[3] Several critics have suggested, though, that Huntington's

view of Islam absolutely conforms to the traditional Orientalist view that Said had depicted.

Critics who were sympathetic to Said's overall thinking generally agreed with his opinion that the way the West had written about the Orient* had indeed allowed the thinking that enabled colonialism to develop. But some did point out gaps and conflicts in Said's ideas and his thinking. Scholars such as the Indian philosopher Gayatri Spivak* have criticized *Orientalism* for failing to take into account both gender and class. Others see Said's humanism*—his rationalist outlook—as outdated.

Responses

Said responded to the critics he saw as more traditionally Orientalist by saying that they had completely misunderstood his point about the relationship between Orientalism and colonialism. He reminded them that *Orientalism* was not just about the content of Orientalist writing, but also about how that content is expressed. He felt they missed his point about the relationship the scholar assumed he had with the Oriental subject.

Said also argued that Orientalists were unwilling to acknowledge what he saw as the clear political dimension of much of their scholarship. He used Napoleon's journey to Egypt in 1798* to argue that research into the Orient* often took place in order to prepare the way for political or economic colonization. Said again stated that his main academic interest in examining Orientalism was the "remarkable parallel between the rise of modern Orientalist scholarship and the acquisition of vast Eastern empires by Britain and France." That, he insisted, was a "crucial point that [Bernard] Lewis refuses to deal with."[4]

Said's most passionate defense of *Orientalism* came as a response to the suggestion that he saw the Occident (the countries of the West) and the Orient (the East) as distinct and separate, when in reality they were part of a continuous sequence and at certain points were not all that different. The point was made by scholars who were sympathetic to Said's views, such as anthropologist James Clifford,* as well as by some who were completely opposed to his arguments like Bernard Lewis. Said hit back by saying that he saw the East as described by Orientalists as something they themselves had constructed. It was based around a geographical understanding they had built themselves that obscured the very real complexities of both human experience and human history.

Conflict and Consensus

Many scholars found inspiration in Said's ideas and went on to both create and then develop the modern field of postcolonial studies.* But the core disagreement between Said's view of colonialism and the view of traditional Orientalists has never been resolved. Now the voices of emerging neoconservatives*—those who think there is currently a deep and fundamental conflict between the Muslim and Arab worlds and Western civilization—have also been added to those who do not accept Said's view.

His most outspoken critics have not shifted much, if at all, in their opposition to his ideas, and it can be said that they became even more sure of their stance after the 9/11* terrorist attacks of 2001.

Said continued to defend his views and focused on responding to what he saw as people's misinterpretations of *Orientalism*. Later, he added an epilogue to the book where he expressed regret over the fact that some groups in the Arab world had used his work to justify an aggressive and rigid form of nationalism. He was also concerned that academia was too focused on language when he felt that the need for rigorous historical analysis was just as important.

Many scholars have been inspired by Said's historical approach that draws from many different disciplines, and have used this means of study to further analyze colonialism and its legacies. A significant amount of this new work focuses on international development, governance, and aid and how these modern activities can, in fact, be seen as the same colonial ideas being expressed in a new form. *Orientalism* has also led to detailed studies that look at how colonial culture and ways of governing actually changed the colonized societies.

NOTES

1   Edward W. Said, Oleg Grabar, and Bernard Lewis, "Orientalism: An Exchange," *New York Review of Books*, August 12, 1982.

2   Bernard Lewis, "The Question of Orientalism," *New York Review of Books*, June 24, 1982.

3   Samuel P. Huntington, *The Clash of Civilizations and the Remaking of World Order*, (New York: Simon and Schuster, 1996).

4   Edward Said, *Orientalism* (New York: Vintage Books, 1978), 343.

MODULE 10
THE EVOLVING DEBATE

KEY POINTS

- *Orientalism*'s most important contribution was to emphasize the enduring impact of colonialism* and its influence on the global political and economic power structures that followed.

- Humanities scholars widely consider *Orientalism* to be the founding text in the field of postcolonial studies.* It set out a framework that academics in fields such as literature, history, art history, and cultural and sexuality studies, have all drawn on.

- *Orientalism* had a significant impact on a large number of prominent academics.

Uses and Problems

Edward Said's *Orientalism* argues that Western academic thinking had a complex relationship with political institutions, and that this was a subject worth studying. Many readers agreed with Said that these relationships were hard to disentangle. For them, Said's thinking identified an important problem. How do you study non-Western societies without reinforcing a view of power that devalues the non-Western subject? Said suggests that the best way to solve the problem is to focus on how these societies are represented, the language that is used in doing so and the way verbal and written interactions create a view of something (i.e. discourse).* This approach, inspired by the French philosopher Michel Foucault,* is an integral part of postcolonial studies.

> 66 The most thought-provoking dimension of the 'new' scholarship on colonial situations, in relation to the 'old', is the way it calls into question the position of the observer, not simply in terms of social biases but in terms of the ways in which forms of knowledge and conceptions of change are themselves shaped by a history of which imperialism* is a central development. 99
>
> Frederick Cooper,* *Colonialism in Question: Theory, Knowledge, History*

Since Said, much academic work on colonialism has focused on how colonial rule created a very particular system of language and concepts to allow the West to organize and understand knowledge. The system was ultimately designed to give approval to those in power. These were, of course, issues that Said raised in *Orientalism*. The Indian philosopher Gayatri Spivak* has defined the colonial "subaltern"* (a person or group considered to be of inferior rank) in terms of their speech. The scholar Homi Bhabha* has argued that hybridity*—the cultural mix that means both colonizers and colonized are not wholly part of one group or another, resulting in social and cultural misunderstandings—is a key feature of coloniality.* All these ideas can be traced back to *Orientalism*.

Said defined Orientalism as a discourse that is there to produce and reproduce global power structures. In doing so he questioned whether decolonization* could really be seen as being a true break with the past. He argues that even under independent rule, European domination persisted. Said's ideas showed how the colonial discourse continues through modern global activities. His book helped to lay the groundwork for further study of the power dynamics that colonialism left behind.

Schools of Thought

Orientalism defined empire* as more than just a system of government and economics. It was a way of seeing the world. Said's primary focus on the notion and effects of empire and colonialism gave rise to modern Western postcolonial studies. This subject looks at many interesting concepts and subgroups, such as subalternity, hybridity, transnationalism* (the fact that people can move about more freely nowadays), and gender and sexuality studies.

Subaltern studies began in the 1980s and was pushed forward at first by a group of South Asian historians who were very critical of the fact that academic history on the Indian subcontinent was driven by colonial and postcolonial works. The aim of subaltern studies is to make the subaltern—the poor, non-white peasant—the center of attention. Despite working with sources that are different from the ones Said used for *Orientalism*, subaltern studies does focus on a number of the same issues. How are Orientals represented? And importantly, who is allowed to represent whom? This makes plain the power issues that come up when the act of representation takes place.

Said focused on what was produced culturally both by and for a European elite to drive his arguments. Subaltern studies puts social and economic class at the center of the postcolonial issue in a way that Said did not. It also brings into question Said's strict division between the colonizer and the colonized by exploring the vital role played by elite members of colonized societies in supporting the colonial project. By doing this, subaltern studies tries to write "history from below" putting the subaltern—the poor, non-white peasant—center stage. This viewpoint had rarely been taken into account in mainstream historical scholarship.[1]

Recent scholars have studied the idea of "regimes of knowledge" that were created by colonial rule. Works like Nicholas Dirks'* *Castes of Mind*,[2] Eric Hobsbawm's* *The Invention of Tradition*,[3] and Max Weiss's* *In the Shadow of Sectarianism*[4] analyze how European colonial administrations brought European understandings of the societies they colonized into their governing processes and organization of social structures. However, these views were often wrong. For example, Dirks argues that the caste system in India is neither as rigid nor as unified as it is often portrayed in the West. It was false assumptions, therefore, that changed colonial societies in ways that continue to have an impact today.

Alongside Said and Gayatri Spivak, Homi Bhabha is considered one of the founders of postcolonial studies. He has examined what he calls the neglected liminality* between the colonizer and the colonized. This is the point where these groups intersect. In *The Location of Culture*,[5] Bhabha studies the anxious, unstable nature of the colonial relationship. In his view, colonial rule is not just about who dominates and who is dominated. It is also an unsettling encounter with the "Other." The colonizer is acutely aware of being "out of place." Even while colonizers have power, they are still dependent on the "native informant." This informant is a non-European government official, who in effect becomes a mirror image of the colonizer himself. Bhabha calls this "mimicry."

Bhabha argues that this colonial anxiety drives the colonizer to constantly want to reinforce his or her identity and emphasize the differences between the colonizer and the colonized. This in turn produces stereotypes that are full of contradictions: "natives" who are oversexed yet impotent, cunning yet intellectually inferior, lazy yet efficient workers. Bhabha calls this area of uncertainty "hybridity." It is a core concept in postcolonial theory, even if not everyone agrees with it.

Scholars have looked at other areas in assessing colonial history. Anthropologist Ann Laura Stoler* has been influential, bringing sexuality and reproduction into her analysis of colonial discourse. In Stoler's view, colonial powers' strict regimes of sexual control reinforced the idea of difference.[6] People who did not fit into what the colonial powers believed to be acceptable categories—for example, mixed-race couples and children—were considered a danger to social stability.

Other scholars such as Lila Abu-Lughod,* Leila Ahmed,* and Deniz Kandiyoti* have focused on gender issues. In works including *Remaking Women: Feminism and Modernity in the Middle East,*[7] *Women and Gender in Islam,*[8] and *Women, Islam and the State,*[9] these scholars have looked at how gender relations also shaped the colonial discourse. When a Victorian idea of domestic femininity was brought into colonized societies, it highlighted more misunderstandings about local culture. Strict Victorian sexual morality created its opposite—the idea of the "backward," oppressed Oriental woman, who needs to be rescued by European values.

Recent scholarship examines the growth of neoliberalism,* a philosophy that believes in free trade and the deregulation of trading and financial markets, and its relation to colonialism. In their book *Empire,*[10] Michael Hardt* and Antonio Negri* argue that in the second half of the twentieth century the old colonialism (a system that was based on an interaction between a powerful country and its colonies) gave way to a more global system of European and American domination. This involved multinational corporations as well as the United Nations,* the World Bank,* and the International Monetary Fund.* Along with Bhabha and Spivak and others, Hardt and Negri are exploring how the old colonial models that Said laid out in *Orientalism* are changing and evolving.

In Current Scholarship

Orientalism is now part of a large body of work in postcolonial studies that includes a wide range of anti-colonial* texts. Some of these were written by authors living in the colonized world during the first half of the twentieth century; others were written during the Cold War* period by those living in former European colonies.

Certain scholars are working further on Said's core idea that Orientalism was a system of thought that brought about Western colonial power. Others are developing new thoughts and ideas to drive the debate forward. Talal Asad's* work on religion in the modern world (particularly *Formations of the Secular: Christianity, Islam, Modernity*)[11] takes a distinctive approach, questioning the view that Western secularism*—a system that is unconnected with spiritual or religious matters—is the only legitimate "modern" way for society to be organized.

Ann Laura Stoler studies how methods of racial and sexual control began in the colonies. Her major works are *Carnal Knowledge and Imperial Power: Race and the Intimate in Colonial Rule,*[12] and *Race and the Education of Desire: Foucault's History of Sexuality and the Colonial Order of Things.*[13] These two books address questions of sexuality and colonialism that Said discusses only briefly in *Orientalism.* Stoler looks at the sexualized language of colonial conquest and examines the way non-Western sexuality has been both demonized and trivialized. Most importantly, she questions the stress colonialism places on the "innate" difference between the colonizer and the colonized.

NOTES

1   Ranajit Guha, ed., *A Subaltern Studies Reader, 1986–1995* (Minneapolis: University of Minnesota Press, 1997).

2   Nicholas Dirks, *Castes of Mind: Colonialism and the Making of Modern India* (Princeton: Princeton University Press, 2001).

3   Eric Hobsbawm and Terence Ranger, eds., *The Invention of Tradition* (Cambridge: Cambridge University Press, 1983).

4   Max Weiss, *In the Shadow of Sectarianism: Law, Shi`ism, and the Making of Modern Lebanon* (Cambridge: Harvard University Press, 2010).

5   Homi Bhabha, *The Location of Culture* (New York: Routledge Press, 1994).

6   Ann Laura Stoler, *Carnal Knowledge and Imperial Power: Race and the Intimate in Colonial Rule* (Berkeley: University of California Press, 2002).

7   Lila Abu-Lughod, ed., *Remaking Women: Feminism and Modernity in the Middle East* (Princeton: Princeton University Press, 1998).

8   Leila Ahmed, *Women and Gender in Islam: Historical Roots of a Modern Debate* (New Haven: Yale University Press, 1992).

9   Deniz Kandiyoti, ed., *Women, Islam and the State* (Basingstoke: Macmillan, 1991).

10   Michael Hardt and Antonio Negri, *Empire* (Boston: Harvard University Press, 2000).

11   Talal Asad, *Formations of the Secular: Christianity, Islam, Modernity* (Stanford: Stanford University Press, 2003).

12   Stoler, *Carnal Knowledge.*

13   Ann Laura Stoler, *Race and the Education of Desire: Foucault's 'History of Sexuality' and the Colonial Order of Things* (Durham: Duke University Press, 1995).

MODULE 11
IMPACT AND INFLUENCE TODAY

KEY POINTS

- *Orientalism* is taught and used widely across the social sciences and humanities and is considered one of the most important twentieth-century works of intellectual history and critical theory.*

- Said's ideas in *Orientalism* continue to challenge the cultural, political, and economic domination of formerly colonized peoples and territories.

- Those responding to the text's challenges fall into two groups: those who reject *Orientalism*'s main arguments as unfairly characterizing the West and the field of Orientalism, and those who seek to use Said's ideas to constructively investigate their own fields, or explore issues related to colonialism* and its aftermath more thoroughly.

Position

Edward Said's *Orientalism* was written as a challenge to the dominant modes of thought in this area. The book discusses a deeply rooted and complex system of global power relations. This means that its central concerns are more relevant than ever in the post-Cold War,* post-9/11* world. As Said pointed out in a later work, *Covering Islam*,[1] Western depictions of Arabs and Islam became more racially stereotyped after the 9/11 attacks. They then intensified during the wars in Iraq and Afghanistan. This has coincided with an increasingly globalized economic system that has increased inequality, with Western countries controlling much of the money while Eastern factories do much of the work. In this context, it is clear that Said's concept of Orientalist discourse is still worthy of discussion.

> 66 What I should like also to have contributed here is a better understanding of the way cultural domination has operated. If this stimulates a new kind of dealing with the Orient, indeed if it eliminates the 'Orient' and the 'Occident' altogether, then we shall have advanced a little in the process of what Raymond Williams has called the 'unlearning' of 'the inherent dominative mode. 99
>
> Edward Said, *Orientalism*

Interaction

Said challenged the idea that scholars could isolate themselves from the people they studied. He said there is an undeniable political relationship between the two. *Orientalism* talks about the importance of looking at the conditions under which scholars study, and examines the fact that they are generally seen as people who tell the truth. This issue was also taken up by Indian philosopher Gayatri Spivak* in "Can the Subaltern Speak?"[2]. The relationship between the scholar and the studied is vitally important and Said's work demands that scholars examine the assumptions they make about their subject.

This is especially important when it is Western scholars studying previously colonized places. *Orientalism* questions the field of "area studies,"* i.e. broad-based study of a defined region, such as African or Middle East studies. It suggests that these are categories that were born out of the colonial era. The Iranian–American scholar Hamid Dabashi* has developed this idea, suggesting that dividing the world into regions defined by the West has created "disposable knowledge." This is because once the political system changes, the category is no longer useful.

According to Dabashi, the lead-up to the United States' war in Afghanistan was an example of this, as knowledge about Afghan history, society, and culture was produced. Scholars like Timothy Mitchell* have applied this idea to international development, aid, and policy issues. They see a discourse that positions the West as "acting" and "saving." In this discourse, "Othered" cultures naturally need help from the superior West. Said's *Orientalism* dealt with issues of the materials scholars produce and the idea that you can't separate knowledge from political power. His work provides a framework and a vocabulary for these schools of thought.

Said took many of his theoretical ideas from poststructuralist* philosophy, the idea that all knowledge is created through discourse.* The French philosopher Michel Foucault's* concept of discourse analysis was especially important. But Said's ideas were different, because he saw everything in terms of its political and historical context. Said felt that the poststructuralist emphasis was too focused on the mechanics of language.

For Said, historical context was absolutely necessary to understand a text. His way of reading tried to look at how a text both reflects and also actively produces the political conditions it is born from. For Said, all scholarly and cultural activity is political by nature. The purpose of reading is to shine a light on how something political is expressed and then taken forward by a text. By challenging some elements of poststructural theory, *Orientalism* made a different approach possible.

The Continuing Debate

Thanks in large part to Edward Said and *Orientalism*, colonialism is now studied for what it can tell us about cultural discourse, politics, and economics. Scholars look at "modernity" and modernization with a critical eye. And the idea that Western secular* modernity is civilization at its best has now been rigorously challenged.

Said said that he was particularly interested in "the extension of post-colonial concerns to the problems of geography."[3] Modern academics like Ammiel Alcalay,* Paul Gilroy,* and Moira Ferguson* have explored this question. They share the approach of Said's *Culture and Imperialism*.[4] Three good examples are Alcalay's *After Jews and Arabs: Remaking Levantine Culture*,[5] Gilroy's *The Black Atlantic: Modernity and Double Consciousness*,[6] and Ferguson's *Subject to Others: British Women Writers and Colonial Slavery, 1670–1834*.[7] All these works look at what is happening in the modern world and its roots in colonialism. They try to offer a new way of seeing the world that doesn't depend on the most important Western texts.

NOTES

1   Edward Said, *Covering Islam: How the Media and the Experts Determine How We See the Rest of the World* (New York: Vintage Books, 1997).

2   Gayatri Chakravorty Spivak, "Can the Subaltern Speak?", in *Marxism and the Interpretation of Culture: International Conference: Selected Papers*, eds. Cary Nelson and Lawrence Grossberg, (Urbana: University of Illinois Press, 1988).

3   Edward Said, *Orientalism* (New York: Vintage Books, 1978), 350.

4   Edward Said, *Culture and Imperialism* (New York: Vintage Books, 1994).

5   Ammiel Alcalay, *After Jews and Arabs: Remaking Levantine Culture* (Minneapolis: University of Minnesota Press, 1992).

6   Paul Gilroy, *The Black Atlantic: Modernity and Double Consciousness* (Cambridge: Harvard University Press, 1993).

7   Moira Ferguson, *Subject to Others: British Women Writers and Colonial Slavery, 1670–1834* (New York: Routledge, 1992).

MODULE 12
WHERE NEXT?

KEY POINTS

- As a text with ongoing political and intellectual relevance, *Orientalism* is likely to continue to be expanded on, reinterpreted, and analyzed by people interested in issues relating to colonialism* and postcoloniality.*

- The analytical tools employed in *Orientalism*—working with a wide interdisciplinary* archive of material, discourse* analysis, integrating political arguments into more abstract philosophy, and critical theory*—will most likely be used by scholars for some time to come.

- *Orientalism* is a text that speaks to a wide range of people—including those who have not traditionally had a voice that is considered "legitimate" or "serious" by mainstream academia.

Potential

Orientalism was published more than 30 years ago, but it is still important today in challenging colonialism and its legacies. Edward Said's work created new ways to understand postcolonial power and cultural discourse.

Said's work was specifically about Middle Eastern and Islamic studies, but it exerts an influence across the broader humanities. His ideas have shaped debate in history, anthropology, and cultural studies, as well as area studies,* which is the broad study of a particular region, for example Middle East studies. New generations of academics continue to reinterpret his work for the present day.

    " If we are to take Said's legacy seriously, then—if we are to learn not only from his writings but just as essentially from the intellectual life that he led—we must take responsibility, publicly, for engaging this new US imperial* formation and its attendant forms of violence and intimidation, both domestic and foreign. And to do so requires that we reintegrate Said's specific intellectual and political engagements with the past and present of empire* in the Middle East* ... and its forms of culture, power, and knowledge. **"**

Nadia Abu El-Haj,* "Edward Said and the Political Present," *American Ethnologist*

Orientalism's importance lies in its original arguments and in the ever-changing political context in which it is read. Said insisted that colonialism shaped the colonizers as well as colonized societies. The effects of this are still being felt all over the world in both Eastern and Western societies. The historian Frederick Cooper* wrote: "Said's influence has been profound and not limited to literary studies ... His approach opened up analysis of a wide array of cultural productions and their representations of difference, power, and progress." Cooper also explained how *Orientalism* "has helped to explain how different kinds of political processes became imaginable or inconceivable."[1]

Most of *Orientalism* discusses how Orientalist thought and European colonialism both developed between the eighteenth century and the early twentieth century. But the book's last section, "Orientalism Now," looks at the ways in which Orientalist discourse is still at work at present. Said insisted that Orientalism did not end when the colonies ended. It is still alive and it is still evolving.

The political environment since 9/11* shows that Said was right about this. Colonialism is still with us. Many people believe that much of America's "War on Terror" was self-declared and a large part of the war has been carried out covertly, both inside America and abroad. This particular war has blurred the lines between military action, policing, and spying. Postcolonial theorists are now analyzing how territory and populations are being classified, racialized, and subjected to surveillance in new ways. Many scholars—among them Sverker Finnström,* Neil Whitehead,* Achille Mbembe* and Mahmood Mamdani*— are working in this area, drawing heavily on *Orientalism* as they do so.

Future Directions

New scholars will most likely continue to use Said's analysis to explore the ways in which gender and sexuality play into the history and evolution of Orientalist thought. Feminist scholars have criticized Said for neglecting this. Ann Laura Stoler* uses Said's theories to examine various aspects of this issue. She has suggested that the modern European idea of "proper" sexuality and family structure was shaped by the colonizers' need to differentiate themselves from the colonized. Stoler investigates how the current situation has led to new forms of sexual policing.

Theorists including Jasbir Puar* are exploring how sexuality formed a core element of colonialist and postcolonialist control. Puar's work builds on Said's view that the figure of the "Oriental" was produced by Europe to define the West as clearly superior. This would then justify colonial intervention. Puar sees the new figure of the "Arab/Muslim terrorist" as an Orientalist stereotype and relates to the Victorian-era idea of the Oriental as a delinquent "monster."[2] She also examines how Western ideas of sexuality are used as a barometer of "modernity." She calls this "homonationalism." Her work draws on Said's ideas about culture, discourse, and hegemony* (the dominance of one party by another) to examine ongoing processes of domination in the present day.

Summary

Edward Said's *Orientalism* has had a profound impact. It changed the study of the humanities and how academics relate to their subject. It also influenced the broader political debate about global power, the legacy of colonialism, and American influence in politics, economics and culture. Indeed it still does so today.

Orientalism helped to create a new conceptual framework and language. This made it possible to look at colonial studies as a study in power. Said's theories gave a voice to the previously colonized, so they could oppose the way they were represented and, in many ways, enslaved. To this extent it is a text of liberation.

Orientalism questioned the supposed objectivity and impartiality that disguised the political and social implications of Orientalist scholarship. In it, Said challenged academics to look at the political context and reflect on their own relationship to their area of study. The book is an argument against a universally accepted way of understanding the world. It is also a call for political accountability. *Orientalism* could not have had such an impact on American academic thinking if it had not itself come from high up in the country's academic system.

Unlike many works of scholarship, *Orientalism* has remained relevant since its publication. As the Cold War* between the United States and the Soviet Union came to an end, global capitalism* was expanding. Colonies were over, but other power dynamics were appearing. Events like the 1979 Iranian Revolution,* the escalation of the Israeli–Palestinian conflict,* and the 9/11 terrorist attacks have kept colonialist concerns very much in the spotlight. The field Said helped to found with *Orientalism*—postcolonial studies—has grown and evolved with the changing times. Said's framework can still be used to analyze how our world is structured and how we can understand this structure. More recent scholars have brought different ideas about class, gender, and race to bear on *Orientalism*'s original arguments. This important work continues to provide a basis for further investigation into empire and its legacies in the modern world.

NOTES

1   Frederick Cooper, *Colonialism in Question: Theory, Knowledge, History* (Berkeley: University of California Press, 2005), 47.

2   Jasbir K. Puar and Amit Rai, "Monster, Terrorist, Fag: The War on Terrorism and the Production of Docile Patriots," *Social Text* 20, no. 3 (2002), 117–48.

GLOSSARY

GLOSSARY OF TERMS

Anti-colonialism: opposition to colonial rule—that is, the system whereby one nation rules over another.

Anti-imperialism: opposition to the system of rule by empire.

Arab–Israeli War (1948): the first Arab–Israeli War. Israel declared its independence on May 14, 1948 and was invaded one day later by Egypt, Syria, Jordan, and Iraq. The Israelis, who had been opposing a revolt aimed at establishing an independent Palestinian state, won the war; over the next three years some 700,000 Palestinian Arabs were either expelled from, or fled, the new country.

Area studies: academic discipline in the post-World War II* American academy, focusing on knowledge produced on the politics, literature, economy, and cultures of a defined geographical area (such as Middle East studies, Latin American studies, African studies, and East Asian studies).

Black September: a Palestinian terrorist organization founded in 1970. The organization was responsible for the 1972 Munich Olympics attacks, in which 11 members of the Israeli Olympic team were kidnaped and killed in a politically motivated action. The group takes its name from an episode in the Jordanian Civil War, which began in September 1970 and led to the expulsion of the Palestinian Liberation Organization (PLO) from Jordan.

Bourgeoisie: the wealthy, capital-owning, upper-middle class in capitalist society. Figures prominently in the work of Karl Marx.

British Mandate: a legal commission set up by the League of Nations in the aftermath of World War I, to administer parts of the former Ottoman empire. The lands, which today comprise Israel, the West Bank, the Gaza Strip, and Jordan, were collectively known as Palestine at the time, and were made subject to British rule. The Mandate Territories were made up of two protectorates: Palestine and Transjordan.

Capitalism: economic and political system in which a country's trade and industry are controlled by private owners for profit, rather than by the state.

Civil rights movement: 1960s movement in the United States that called for an end to racial segregation.

Cold War (1947–91): sustained political tension between the capitalist, US-dominated West and communist USSR (Union of Soviet Socialist Republics) and its allies, creating a bipolar world-power system that largely determined global politics for its duration.

Colonialism: establishment, exploitation, maintenance, acquisition, and expansion of colonies in one territory by people from another territory. Results in a set of unequal relationships between the colonial power and the colony, and often between the colonists and the native population.

Coloniality: the legacy that colonialism imparts in a society. Coloniality refers to the psychological, rather than the physical, products of capitalism. These products include attitudes, racial and social prejudices, and social and caste structures. They are derived from systems of knowledge produced by the colonial power and imposed on the colonized.

Counter-hegemonic: thought that attempts to question, challenge, and subvert dominant systems of power and the associated ways of understanding the world.

Critical theory: body of philosophy with a strong Marxist* influence that seeks to critique twentieth- and twenty-first-century society and culture.

Decolonization: the process of being freed from colonial rule.

Deconstruction: the method of taking apart texts in order to find their hidden meanings. Deconstruction assumes words have meanings only in relation to one another. For example, red is red because it is not any other color. If words have meanings because they contrast to one another, then the words an author chooses to put together show the beliefs and choices that author makes in expressing their views.

Disciplinary power: Michel Foucault's concept of disciplinary power suggests that a dominant group exerts authority over its subjects or subordinates by credibly threatening to punish any who attempt to exceed the bounds imposed on them. An example would be the disciplinary power wielded by prison guards over prisoners.

Discourse (Foucauldian discourse): French philosopher Michel Foucault's concept of a large system of interrelated signs created through verbal interaction in societies. Discourse is an ever-expanding body of knowledge, articulated in a particular vocabulary, which defines the way in which the world can be "known" and understood.

Discursive formation: a term in discourse analysis. It describes the communications (written, spoken, performed, etc.) that form discourses to be analyzed.

Empire: an extensive group of states or countries under a single supreme authority. Said focuses particularly on the leading European empires of the nineteenth century, such as the French and British empires that colonized large territories of the Islamic world.

Epistemology: the theory of knowledge.

Frankfurt School (critical theory): a school of philosophy of the 1920s whose followers were involved in a reappraisal of Marxism, particularly in terms of the cultural and aesthetic dimension of modern industrial society. Principal figures include Theodor Adorno, Max Horkheimer, and Herbert Marcuse.

Geographic-temporal imagination: Said proposes that a location or a people exist not only in reality, but also as an artificial construct shaped by unifying or dominant views of geography and history, reinforced by stories, maps, and descriptive imagery.

Hegemony: the dominance of one party by another, which includes indirect forms of domination, such as the dominant party holding the exclusive right to set social norms and assume the role of leader.

Humanism: rationalist outlook or system of thought attaching prime importance to human rather than divine or supernatural matters.

Hybridity: Homi Bhabha's concept of the fundamental anxiety and instability at the heart of the colonial encounter, the space between colonizer and colonized in which identity and power are established and contested.

Imperial: of or relating to an empire. Said uses the term with particular emphasis to the power and domination represented by the empire and the process of colonization.

Interdisciplinary: relating to more than one branch of knowledge.

International Monetary Fund (IMF): an organization of 188 countries, based in Washington, D.C., that promotes global financial stability. It lends money to heavily indebted countries when no one else will.

Iranian Revolution (1979): revolt that ousted Western-backed Shah Mohammad Reza Pahlavi (the ruler of Iran at the time) and saw the establishment of an Islamic Republic led by Shi'a religious leader Ayatollah Ruhollah Khomeini.

Israeli–Palestinian conflict: tension that arguably originated with the 1948 expulsion of most of the Palestinian Arab population from present-day Israel. It has seen several intensifications over the past three decades, including the Israeli invasion of Lebanon in 1982 and two intifadas (Palestinian uprisings): one in 1987–91 and another in 2000–5.

Liminality: state of being between or on the borders of (but not wholly a part of) groups, definitions, or identities.

Linguistics: the study of human speech in all its aspects.

Marxism: an approach to social science based on materialism, history, and class, founded by Karl Marx in the nineteenth century. It views everything as reflective of an eternal class struggle, with the goal of transforming society into a classless utopia (perfect place). Forms of Marxism remain popular today.

Middle East: an extensive area of southwestern Asia and northern Africa, stretching from the Mediterranean Sea to Pakistan and including the Arabian Peninsula. Also known as the Near East in historical contexts.

Napoleon's expedition to Egypt (1798–1801): Napoleon Bonaparte of France invaded Egypt in order to wrest the region from British influence. He also brought a group of intellectuals with him to spread scientific learning and Enlightenment ideas.

Near Eastern: a term generally applied to the countries of southwestern Asia between the Mediterranean Sea and India, also called the "Middle East." The term is especially used in historical contexts.

Négritude: literary and intellectual movement originated by black, French-speaking thinkers and writers in the 1930s. It centered on blackness as a shared collective identity and rejected French colonialism.

Neoconservatism: school of political thought that emerged in the American academy in the 1960s and continued to evolve throughout the latter half of the twentieth century. It was characterized by a championing of democracy and US-national interests, brought about through military intervention if necessary, and a belief that the Muslim and Arab worlds constitute the principal opponents of Western civilization.

Neoliberalism: economic and political philosophy that advocates free trade, the deregulation of markets, and the rollback of the liberal welfare state.

9/11: the hijacking of four passenger airliners in the United States by 19 individuals affiliated with the al-Qaeda terrorist organization. Two planes were flown into the World Trade Center towers in New York City and one into the Pentagon military headquarters in Washington, DC on September 11, 2001, resulting in significant loss of life.

Orient: the countries of Asia, including those of the Middle East. Said juxtaposes this term with the "West" or "Occident," which encompasses Europe and North America.

Palestine issue: *see* Israeli–Palestinian conflict.

Paternalism: policy or practise on the part of people in authority of restricting the freedom and responsibilities of those subordinate to or otherwise dependent on them in their supposed interest.

Postcolonial studies, postcolonialism, postcolonial theory: academic disciplines that critically examine the cultural, political, economic, and social process of colonialism and its legacies.

Poststructuralism: loosely defined intellectual movement of the mid- to late-twentieth century that pushed back against the early-twentieth-century structuralist movement's contention that knowledge is formed in binaries (for example, male/female, East/ West). Broadly, it argues that all knowledge is created through discourse and is by definition ever changing and unstable. Prominent philosophers (not all of whom accept the poststructuralist label) include Michel Foucault, Julia Kristeva, Jean Baudrillard, and Jacques Derrida.

Proletariat: laboring, wage-earning class in capitalist society. The term is derived from the politico-economic thought of Karl Marx.

Secular: unconnected with spiritual or religious matters.

Six-Day War: a 1967 conflict sparked by an attack on Israel by Egypt, Syria, and Jordan. The Israelis survived initial losses to win the war, thanks largely to their access to American military technology.

Subaltern: any person or group of inferior rank and station, whether because of race, class, gender, sexual orientation, ethnicity, or religion.

Textuality: an idea in linguistics and literary theory. It is a characteristic of a text (i.e. an object under study) that communicates meaning. A text's textuality is never set in stone; given aspects of a text have more or less textuality at given times to given people.

Transnationalism: social phenomenon and scholarly research agenda resulting from the rise in global connections between people and the decreasing importance of economic and social boundaries between nations.

United Nations: an organization of 193 countries, established in 1945 to promote world peace and cooperation among nations.

Vietnam War: a 20-year war (1955–75) fought between the Communist Northern Vietnamese and the South Vietnamese, who were heavily backed by the United States, which deployed its forces in 1964. The protracted conflict had a major impact on American politics, most notably with the rise of the anti-war movement, part of the larger counterculture movement of the 1960s. The Vietnam War led many scholars to examine the notion of an "American empire" and the history and legacy of empires more generally.

World Bank: the International Bank for Reconstruction and Development, known as the World Bank, is an organization of 188 countries, based in Washington, D.C., that assists low- and middle-income countries to reduce poverty and develop their economies.

World systems theory: an approach to world history associated with Immanuel Wallerstein. It sees a "division of labor" imposed on the world, with "core" states focusing on lucrative, high-skill work, and "peripheral" states focusing on intensive, low-pay work.

World War I (1914–18): an international conflict centered in Europe and involving the major economic world powers of the day.

World War II (1939–45): global war between the vast majority of world states, including all great powers of the time.

Yom Kippur War (1973): War fought between Israel and a coalition of Arab states. Fighting broke out on October 6, 1973 (the Jewish holy day of Yom Kippur) and continued until October 25.

PEOPLE MENTIONED IN THE TEXT

Anouar Abdel-Malek (1924–2012) was an Egyptian–French professor of political science. He believed passionately that Arab nations in North Africa and the Middle East should unite as one—he was a pan-Arabist. Although he studied philosophy as a student, he became a prominent political scientist from 1970 as head of Paris's premier research institute, the Centre Nationale de la Recherche Scientifique (National Centre for Scientific Research).

Nadia Abu El Haj (b. 1962) is a Palestinian–American anthropologist who currently teaches at Barnard College in New York City. Her work has focused on the intersection of modern scientific disciplines (such as archaeology and genetics) and racial, ethnic, and national identity.

Ibrahim Abu-Lughod (1929–2001) was a Palestinian–American political scientist who was a professor at Northwestern University. Said dedicated *Orientalism* to him as an acknowledgment of his work in the field.

Lila Abu-Lughod (b. 1952) is a Palestinian–American anthropologist at Columbia University whose work has been highly influential in gender, Middle East, and postcolonial studies.* Her more prominent works include *Veiled Sentiments: Honor and Poetry in a Bedouin Society* and *Do Muslim Women Need Saving?*

Eqbal Ahmad (1933–99) was a Pakistani political scientist, writer, journalist, and anti-war activist. He argued that colonial powers misused their position for economic gain.

Leila Ahmed (b. 1940) is an Egyptian–American scholar of Middle East history and gender studies at Harvard University. Her work on gender in Islam has been notably influential; she is best known for her book, *Women and Gender in Islam: Historical Roots of a Modern Debate*.

Ammiel Alcalay (b. 1956) is assistant professor of classical and Oriental literatures at Queens College (City University of New York). As a poet, translator, writer, and critic, he has written widely on literary and historical politics in the cultures of the Mediterranean.

Idi Amin (1925–2003) was the third President of Uganda. His authoritarian rule of Uganda (between 1971 and 1979) was characterized by corruption, human rights abuses, and mass murder.

Talal Asad (b. 1933) is an anthropologist at the City University of New York (CUNY). He has made a major contribution to postcolonial theory, in particular calling for a re-examination of secularism.

Jane Austen (1775–1817) was a British writer known for her novels on English upper-class social mores, including *Pride and Prejudice* and *Sense and Sensibility*. Her depictions of Orientalism have come under scrutiny by postcolonial scholars.

Homi Bhabha (b. 1949) is a cultural studies scholar at Harvard University and one of the most important figures in postcolonial studies* (along with Said and Gayatri Spivak). His best-known work is his 1994 collection of essays, *The Location of Culture*, in which he established such influential concepts as mimicry and hybridity.*

Aimé Césaire (1913–2008) was a poet, playwright, author, and political activist from Martinique. He helped found the French-speaking Négritude* movement in colonial literature that sought to affirm black solidarity and identity in the face of racist French colonial ideology.

James Clifford (b. 1945) is an American historian at the University of California at Santa Cruz. He is best known for his critical work in the field of anthropology.

Joseph Conrad (1857–1924) was a Polish author who settled in England. He is best known for his novella about Belgian colonialism* in the Congo, *Heart of Darkness*.

Frederick Cooper (b. 1947) is an American historian and currently a professor of history at New York University. He is best known for his work in colonization, decolonization, and African history.

Hamid Dabashi (b. 1951) is an Iranian–American postcolonial and cultural studies scholar at Columbia University and a former colleague of Said's. His work, including *Brown Skin, White Masks, Iran: A People Interrupted* and *Post-Orientalism: Knowledge and Power in Time of Terror*, follows in Said's interdisciplinary* mold, and deals with questions of identity and power in the postcolonial world.

Jacques Derrida (1930–2004) was a French philosopher and critical theorist, founder of the "deconstructionist" idea. Deconstruction is all about finding the multiple meanings in a text, many of which the original author may not have intended and which have a tendency to shift and change based on context and reader. Derrida applied his methodology to all forms of art, academia, and other cultural communications.

Nicholas Dirks (b. 1950) is currently the Chancellor of the

University of California, Berkeley. He is a champion of postcolonialism and the author of numerous books on South Asian history and culture.

Frantz Fanon (1925–61) was a Martinique-born psychiatrist and philosopher known for his work on the psychological effect of colonialism on the colonized. He called for anti-colonial revolution as the only means by which the colonized could free themselves; his best-known works are *The Wretched of the Earth* and *Black Skin, White Masks*.

Moira Ferguson is James E. Ryan Chair in English and women's literature at the University of Nebraska, Lincoln. Her work, *Subject to Others: British Women Writers and Colonial Slavery, 1670–1834*, explores gender under colonial rule.

Sverker Finnström (b. 1970) is a senior lecturer at the department of cultural anthropology and ethnology at Uppsala University in Sweden. His work draws on Said's *Orientalism*.

Gustave Flaubert (1821–80) was a prominent French author best known for his novel *Madame Bovary*. Said discusses Flaubert's writings on the Orient in great length in *Orientalism*.

Michel Foucault (1926–84) was a French poststructuralist* philosopher best known for his theories on knowledge production, power, sexuality, and modern forms of governance and social control. His works were an inspiration for Said.

Sigmund Freud (1856–1939) was an Austrian psychologist known for founding the field of modern psychoanalysis, which treats psychological issues through dialogue in an attempt to unearth our basic drives and memories.

Paul Gilroy (b. 1956) is a professor of American and English Literature at King's College London. He has a particular interest in postcolonial studies.

Antonio Gramsci (1891–1937) was an Italian communist writer and political philosopher, best known for his theory on hegemony. Gramsci argued that the bourgeois ruling (producing) class in society must manufacture consent to its rule; this consent and its supporting structures are called hegemony.

Michael Hardt (b. 1960) is an American political philosopher and literary theorist. He is best known for the work *Empire* that he co-wrote with Antonio Negri.

Eric Hobsbawm (1917–2012) was an Egyptian-born British Marxist historian. He wrote widely on the rise of industrial capitalism,* socialism, and nationalism and was one of Britain's foremost historians.

Samuel Huntington (1927–2008) was a conservative American political scientist, author of the hotly debated, post-Cold War* text, *The Clash of Civilizations and the Remaking of World Order*.

Deniz Kandiyoti (b. 1944) is a scholar in Middle East and gender studies at the School of Oriental and African Studies in London. Her work includes *Women, Islam, and the State* and *Gendering the Middle East: Emerging Perspectives*.

T. E. Lawrence (1888–1935) was a British army officer who famously participated in the 1916–18 Arab revolt against Ottoman rule and exemplified the colonial stereotype of the colonizer "gone native" (i.e. assimilated into the society of the colonized). His story was the basis of the film, *Lawrence of Arabia*, released in 1962 to great acclaim.

Bernard Lewis (b. 1916) is a British–American historian and professor emeritus of Islamic history at Princeton University. He is considered one of the most influential Western scholars of the Middle East.

Mahmood Mamdani (b. 1946) is a Ugandan academic and director of the Makerere Institute of Social Research, as well as the Herbert Lehman professor of government at the School of International and Public Affairs and the professor of anthropology, political science, and African studies at Columbia University. He specializes in African politics and history and a number of his works have explored colonialism and its legacy.

Louis Massignon (1883–1962) was a Catholic scholar of Islam, instrumental in getting Islam recognized by Catholics as an Abrahamic faith. His work was studied by Said as a basis for *Orientalism*.

Achille Mbembe (b. 1957) is a philosopher and political scientist at the University of the Witwatersrand in Johannesburg, South Africa. His work draws heavily on Said's *Orientalism*.

Albert Memmi (b. 1920) is a Tunisian Jewish writer best known for his novel, *The Pillar of Salt,* and his philosophical work, *The Colonizer and the Colonized*, which analyzed the psychology of the complex relationship between colonizer and colonized.

Timothy Mitchell (b. 1955) is a British political scientist and postcolonial scholar at Columbia University. His work focuses on Egypt and the development of governance structures during the colonial and postcolonial periods. Important works include *Colonising*

Egypt and *Rule of Experts: Egypt, Techno-Politics, Modernity.*

Jean Mohr (b. 1925) is a Swiss documentary photographer. He has worked with some of the world's major humanitarian organizations, including the United Nations High Commission for Refugees and the International Committee of the Red Cross (ICRC).

Robert Mugabe (b. 1924) is the current President of Zimbabwe, having assumed office in 1987. He rules Zimbabwe as a one-party state and has been accused of gross human rights violations in the country.

Antonio Negri (b. 1933) is an Italian Marxist sociologist and political philosopher. He is best known for the work *Empire* that he co-wrote with Michael Hardt.

Jasbir Puar is associate professor of women's and gender studies at Rutgers University. She is known for her work on queer theory and studies into how sexuality was used as a means of control by colonial powers.

Ernest Renan (1823–92) was a French philosopher and writer. He was an expert in Middle Eastern languages and civilizations.

Maxime Rodinson (1915–2004) was a French Marxist historian and sociologist. As an Orientalist scholar, his work centered on Islamic culture, particularly the prophet Mohammed, and he acquired a reputation for his outspoken commentary on Middle Eastern affairs.

Silvestre de Sacy (1758–1838) was a French linguist, writer, and Orientalist. Said studied his work to explore the origins of Orientalism.

Jean-Paul Sartre (1905–80) was a French philosopher and writer and key figure in twentieth-century philosophy and Marxism. His work had a considerable influence on postcolonial studies.

R. W. Southern (1912–2001) was a celebrated English medieval historian who spent most of his career at the University of Oxford and was a popular and influential historian with students and the public. Among his most renowned works is *The Making of the Middle Ages* (1953).

Gayatri Spivak (b. 1942) is an Indian philosopher and critical theorist at Columbia University, and one of the key figures of postcolonial studies.* She is best known for her work critiquing European systems of knowledge production and their silencing of subaltern* voices—a theme she explored in depth in her seminal essay "Can the Subaltern Speak?"

Ann Laura Stoler (b. 1949) is an American anthropologist at the New School (New York City). She is best known for her work on sexuality, empire, and postcoloniality.

A. L. Tibawi (1910–81) is a Palestinian historian. He studied in Jerusalem before the formation of the modern state of Israel in 1948. He then left the Middle East for London, where he set up a fund to support Palestinian students made homeless by the creation of the Israeli state while he was working at the University of London. His life's work focused on the international relations and diplomatic history between the West (Europe and the USA) and the Middle East.

Immanuel Wallerstein (b. 1930) is an American sociologist and senior research scholar at Yale University. He is known for his work on the world systems theory.

Max Weiss is an American scholar, translator, and associate professor of history and Near Eastern studies at Princeton University. He specializes in the culture and history of the Middle East.

Neil Whitehead (1956–2012) was an English anthropologist and former professor of anthropology at the University of Wisconsin-Madison. He is known primarily for his work exploring the anthropology of violence, post-human anthropology, and studies on South America and the Caribbean.

William Butler Yeats (1865–1939) was an Irish poet and one of the foremost poets of the twentieth century. Said used his poetry to demonstrate how Orientalist ways of thinking had impacted Western literature.

WORKS CITED

WORKS CITED

Abu El-Haj, Nadia. "Edward Said and the Political Present." *American Ethnologist* 32, no.4 (November 2004): 538–55.

Abu-Lughod, Lila, ed. *Remaking Women: Feminism and Modernity in the Middle East*. Princeton: Princeton University Press, 1998.

Ahmed, Lila. *Women and Gender in Islam: Historical Roots of a Modern Debate*. New Haven: Yale University Press, 1992.

Alcalay, Ammiel. *After Jews and Arabs: Remaking Levantine Culture*. Minneapolis: University of Minnesota Press, 1992.

Asad, Talal. *Formations of the Secular: Christianity, Islam, Modernity*. Stanford: Stanford University Press, 2003.

———. "Review: *Orientalism* by Edward Said." *The English Historical Review* 95.376 (July 1980), 648–9.

Bengelsdorf, Carollee, Margaret Cerullo, and Yogesh Chandrani, eds. *The Selected Writings of Eqbal Ahmad*. New York: Columbia University Press, 2006.

Bhabha, Homi. *The Location of Culture*. New York: Routledge Press, 1994.

Césaire, Aimé. *Discourse on Colonialism*. Translated by Joan Pinkham. London & New York: Monthly Review Press, 1972.

Cooper, Frederick. *Africa Since 1940: The Past of the Present*. New York: Cambridge University Press, 2002.

———. *Colonialism in Question: Theory, Knowledge, History*. Berkeley: University of California Press, 2005.

Dirks, Nicholas. *Castes of Mind: Colonialism and the Making of Modern India*. Princeton: Princeton University Press, 2001.

Ferguson, Moira. *Subject to Others: British Women Writers and Colonial Slavery, 1670–1834*. New York: Routledge, 1992.

Finnström, Sverker and Neil Whitehead, eds. *Virtual War and Magical Death: Technologies and Imaginaries for Terror and Killing*. Durham: Duke University Press, 2013.

Foucault, Michel. *The Archaeology of Knowledge*. Translated by A. M. Sheridan Smith. London: Tavistock Publications, 1972.

———. *Discipline and Punish: The Birth of the Prison*. Translated by Alan

Sheridan. New York: Vintage Books, 1975.

Gilroy, Paul. *The Black Atlantic: Modernity and Double Consciousness*. Cambridge: Harvard University Press, 1993.

Guha, Ranajit, ed. *A Subaltern Studies Reader, 1986–1995*. Minneapolis: University of Minnesota Press, 1997.

Hardt, Michael and Antonio Negri. *Empire*. Cambridge: Harvard University Press, 2000.

Hobsbawm, Eric and Terence Ranger, eds. *The Invention of Tradition*. Cambridge: Cambridge University Press, 1983.

Huntington, Samuel P. *The Clash of Civilizations and the Remaking of World Order*. New York: Simon and Schuster, 1996.

Kandiyoti, Deniz, ed. *Women, Islam and the State*. Basingstoke: Macmillan, 1991.

Lewis, Bernard. "The Question of Orientalism." *New York Review of Books*, June 24, 1982.

Ludden, David. *Reading Subaltern Studies: Critical History, Contested Meaning, and the Globalization of South Asia*. London: Anthem Press, 2002.

Mamdani, Mahmood. *Good Muslim, Bad Muslim: America, the Cold War, and the Roots of Terror.* New York: Pantheon Books, 2004.

Memmi, Albert. *The Colonizer and the Colonized*. London: The Orion Press, 1965.

Puar, Jasbir and Amit Rai. "Monster, Terrorist, Fag: The War on Terrorism and the Production of Docile Patriots." *Social Text* 20, no. 3 (2002): 117–48.

Puar, Jasbir. *Terrorist Assemblages: Homonationalism in Queer Times*. Durham: Duke University Press, 2007.

Razzaz, Munif and Ibrahim Abu-Lughod. *The Evolution of the Meaning of Nationalism*. New York: Doubleday, 1963.

Said, Edward. *Beginnings: Intentions and Method*. New York: Columbia University Press, 1985.

———. *Covering Islam: How the Media and the Experts Determine How We See the Rest of the World*. New York: Vintage Books, 1997.

———. *Joseph Conrad and the Fiction of Autobiography*. Cambridge: Harvard University Press, 1966.

———. *Orientalism*. New York: Vintage Books, 1978.

———. *Out of Place: A Memoir*. New York: Knopf, 1999.

———. *The Politics of Dispossession: The Struggle for Palestinian Self-Determination 1969–1994*. New York: Pantheon Books, 1994.

———. *The Question of Palestine*. New York: Vintage Books, 1979.

———. "Zionism from the Standpoint of Its Victims." *Social Text* 1 (1979), 7–58.

Spivak, Gayatri Chakravorty. "Can the Subaltern Speak?" In *Marxism and the Interpretation of Culture: International Conference: Selected Papers*, edited by Cary Nelson and Lawrence Grossberg, 271–313. Urbana: University of Illinois Press, 1988.

Stoler, Ann Laura. *Carnal Knowledge and Imperial Power: Race and the Intimate in Colonial Rule*. Berkeley: University of California Press, 2002.

———. *Race and the Education of Desire: Foucault's History of Sexuality and the Colonial Order of Things*. Durham: Duke University Press, 1995.

Weiss, Max. *In the Shadow of Sectarianism: Law, Shi`ism, and the Making of Modern Lebanon*. Cambridge: Harvard University Press, 2010.

THE MACAT LIBRARY
BY DISCIPLINE

The Macat Library By Discipline

AFRICANA STUDIES

Chinua Achebe's *An Image of Africa: Racism in Conrad's Heart of Darkness*
W. E. B. Du Bois's *The Souls of Black Folk*
Zora Neale Huston's *Characteristics of Negro Expression*
Martin Luther King Jr's *Why We Can't Wait*
Toni Morrison's *Playing in the Dark: Whiteness in the American Literary Imagination*

ANTHROPOLOGY

Arjun Appadurai's *Modernity at Large: Cultural Dimensions of Globalisation*
Philippe Ariès's *Centuries of Childhood*
Franz Boas's *Race, Language and Culture*
Kim Chan & Renée Mauborgne's *Blue Ocean Strategy*
Jared Diamond's *Guns, Germs & Steel: the Fate of Human Societies*
Jared Diamond's *Collapse: How Societies Choose to Fail or Survive*
E. E. Evans-Pritchard's *Witchcraft, Oracles and Magic Among the Azande*
James Ferguson's *The Anti-Politics Machine*
Clifford Geertz's *The Interpretation of Cultures*
David Graeber's *Debt: the First 5000 Years*
Karen Ho's *Liquidated: An Ethnography of Wall Street*
Geert Hofstede's *Culture's Consequences: Comparing Values, Behaviors, Institutes and Organizations across Nations*
Claude Lévi-Strauss's *Structural Anthropology*
Jay Macleod's *Ain't No Makin' It: Aspirations and Attainment in a Low-Income Neighborhood*
Saba Mahmood's *The Politics of Piety: The Islamic Revival and the Feminist Subject*
Marcel Mauss's *The Gift*

BUSINESS

Jean Lave & Etienne Wenger's *Situated Learning*
Theodore Levitt's *Marketing Myopia*
Burton G. Malkiel's *A Random Walk Down Wall Street*
Douglas McGregor's *The Human Side of Enterprise*
Michael Porter's *Competitive Strategy: Creating and Sustaining Superior Performance*
John Kotter's *Leading Change*
C. K. Prahalad & Gary Hamel's *The Core Competence of the Corporation*

CRIMINOLOGY

Michelle Alexander's *The New Jim Crow: Mass Incarceration in the Age of Colorblindness*
Michael R. Gottfredson & Travis Hirschi's *A General Theory of Crime*
Richard Herrnstein & Charles A. Murray's *The Bell Curve: Intelligence and Class Structure in American Life*
Elizabeth Loftus's *Eyewitness Testimony*
Jay Macleod's *Ain't No Makin' It: Aspirations and Attainment in a Low-Income Neighborhood*
Philip Zimbardo's *The Lucifer Effect*

ECONOMICS

Janet Abu-Lughod's *Before European Hegemony*
Ha-Joon Chang's *Kicking Away the Ladder*
David Brion Davis's *The Problem of Slavery in the Age of Revolution*
Milton Friedman's *The Role of Monetary Policy*
Milton Friedman's *Capitalism and Freedom*
David Graeber's *Debt: the First 5000 Years*
Friedrich Hayek's *The Road to Serfdom*
Karen Ho's *Liquidated: An Ethnography of Wall Street*

John Maynard Keynes's *The General Theory of Employment, Interest and Money*
Charles P. Kindleberger's *Manias, Panics and Crashes*
Robert Lucas's *Why Doesn't Capital Flow from Rich to Poor Countries?*
Burton G. Malkiel's *A Random Walk Down Wall Street*
Thomas Robert Malthus's *An Essay on the Principle of Population*
Karl Marx's *Capital*
Thomas Piketty's *Capital in the Twenty-First Century*
Amartya Sen's *Development as Freedom*
Adam Smith's *The Wealth of Nations*
Nassim Nicholas Taleb's *The Black Swan: The Impact of the Highly Improbable*
Amos Tversky's & Daniel Kahneman's *Judgment under Uncertainty: Heuristics and Biases*
Mahbub Ul Haq's *Reflections on Human Development*
Max Weber's *The Protestant Ethic and the Spirit of Capitalism*

FEMINISM AND GENDER STUDIES

Judith Butler's *Gender Trouble*
Simone De Beauvoir's *The Second Sex*
Michel Foucault's *History of Sexuality*
Betty Friedan's *The Feminine Mystique*
Saba Mahmood's *The Politics of Piety: The Islamic Revival and the Feminist Subject*
Joan Wallach Scott's *Gender and the Politics of History*
Mary Wollstonecraft's *A Vindication of the Rights of Woman*
Virginia Woolf's *A Room of One's Own*

GEOGRAPHY

The Brundtland Report's *Our Common Future*
Rachel Carson's *Silent Spring*
Charles Darwin's *On the Origin of Species*
James Ferguson's *The Anti-Politics Machine*
Jane Jacobs's *The Death and Life of Great American Cities*
James Lovelock's *Gaia: A New Look at Life on Earth*
Amartya Sen's *Development as Freedom*
Mathis Wackernagel & William Rees's *Our Ecological Footprint*

HISTORY

Janet Abu-Lughod's *Before European Hegemony*
Benedict Anderson's *Imagined Communities*
Bernard Bailyn's *The Ideological Origins of the American Revolution*
Hanna Batatu's *The Old Social Classes And The Revolutionary Movements Of Iraq*
Christopher Browning's *Ordinary Men: Reserve Police Batallion 101 and the Final Solution in Poland*
Edmund Burke's *Reflections on the Revolution in France*
William Cronon's *Nature's Metropolis: Chicago And The Great West*
Alfred W. Crosby's *The Columbian Exchange*
Hamid Dabashi's *Iran: A People Interrupted*
David Brion Davis's *The Problem of Slavery in the Age of Revolution*
Nathalie Zemon Davis's *The Return of Martin Guerre*
Jared Diamond's *Guns, Germs & Steel: the Fate of Human Societies*
Frank Dikotter's *Mao's Great Famine*
John W Dower's *War Without Mercy: Race And Power In The Pacific War*
W. E. B. Du Bois's *The Souls of Black Folk*
Richard J. Evans's *In Defence of History*
Lucien Febvre's *The Problem of Unbelief in the 16th Century*
Sheila Fitzpatrick's *Everyday Stalinism*

Eric Foner's *Reconstruction: America's Unfinished Revolution, 1863-1877*
Michel Foucault's *Discipline and Punish*
Michel Foucault's *History of Sexuality*
Francis Fukuyama's *The End of History and the Last Man*
John Lewis Gaddis's *We Now Know: Rethinking Cold War History*
Ernest Gellner's *Nations and Nationalism*
Eugene Genovese's *Roll, Jordan, Roll: The World the Slaves Made*
Carlo Ginzburg's *The Night Battles*
Daniel Goldhagen's *Hitler's Willing Executioners*
Jack Goldstone's *Revolution and Rebellion in the Early Modern World*
Antonio Gramsci's *The Prison Notebooks*
Alexander Hamilton, John Jay & James Madison's *The Federalist Papers*
Christopher Hill's *The World Turned Upside Down*
Carole Hillenbrand's *The Crusades: Islamic Perspectives*
Thomas Hobbes's *Leviathan*
Eric Hobsbawm's *The Age Of Revolution*
John A. Hobson's *Imperialism: A Study*
Albert Hourani's *History of the Arab Peoples*
Samuel P. Huntington's *The Clash of Civilizations and the Remaking of World Order*
C. L. R. James's *The Black Jacobins*
Tony Judt's *Postwar: A History of Europe Since 1945*
Ernst Kantorowicz's *The King's Two Bodies: A Study in Medieval Political Theology*
Paul Kennedy's *The Rise and Fall of the Great Powers*
Ian Kershaw's *The "Hitler Myth": Image and Reality in the Third Reich*
John Maynard Keynes's *The General Theory of Employment, Interest and Money*
Charles P. Kindleberger's *Manias, Panics and Crashes*
Martin Luther King Jr's *Why We Can't Wait*
Henry Kissinger's *World Order: Reflections on the Character of Nations and the Course of History*
Thomas Kuhn's *The Structure of Scientific Revolutions*
Georges Lefebvre's *The Coming of the French Revolution*
John Locke's *Two Treatises of Government*
Niccolò Machiavelli's *The Prince*
Thomas Robert Malthus's *An Essay on the Principle of Population*
Mahmood Mamdani's *Citizen and Subject: Contemporary Africa And The Legacy Of Late Colonialism*
Karl Marx's *Capital*
Stanley Milgram's *Obedience to Authority*
John Stuart Mill's *On Liberty*
Thomas Paine's *Common Sense*
Thomas Paine's *Rights of Man*
Geoffrey Parker's *Global Crisis: War, Climate Change and Catastrophe in the Seventeenth Century*
Jonathan Riley-Smith's *The First Crusade and the Idea of Crusading*
Jean-Jacques Rousseau's *The Social Contract*
Joan Wallach Scott's *Gender and the Politics of History*
Theda Skocpol's *States and Social Revolutions*
Adam Smith's *The Wealth of Nations*
Timothy Snyder's *Bloodlands: Europe Between Hitler and Stalin*
Sun Tzu's *The Art of War*
Keith Thomas's *Religion and the Decline of Magic*
Thucydides's *The History of the Peloponnesian War*
Frederick Jackson Turner's *The Significance of the Frontier in American History*
Odd Arne Westad's *The Global Cold War: Third World Interventions And The Making Of Our Times*

The Macat Library By Discipline

LITERATURE

Chinua Achebe's *An Image of Africa: Racism in Conrad's Heart of Darkness*
Roland Barthes's *Mythologies*
Homi K. Bhabha's *The Location of Culture*
Judith Butler's *Gender Trouble*
Simone De Beauvoir's *The Second Sex*
Ferdinand De Saussure's *Course in General Linguistics*
T. S. Eliot's *The Sacred Wood: Essays on Poetry and Criticism*
Zora Neale Huston's *Characteristics of Negro Expression*
Toni Morrison's *Playing in the Dark: Whiteness in the American Literary Imagination*
Edward Said's *Orientalism*
Gayatri Chakravorty Spivak's *Can the Subaltern Speak?*
Mary Wollstonecraft's *A Vindication of the Rights of Women*
Virginia Woolf's *A Room of One's Own*

PHILOSOPHY

Elizabeth Anscombe's *Modern Moral Philosophy*
Hannah Arendt's *The Human Condition*
Aristotle's *Metaphysics*
Aristotle's *Nicomachean Ethics*
Edmund Gettier's *Is Justified True Belief Knowledge?*
Georg Wilhelm Friedrich Hegel's *Phenomenology of Spirit*
David Hume's *Dialogues Concerning Natural Religion*
David Hume's *The Enquiry for Human Understanding*
Immanuel Kant's *Religion within the Boundaries of Mere Reason*
Immanuel Kant's *Critique of Pure Reason*
Søren Kierkegaard's *The Sickness Unto Death*
Søren Kierkegaard's *Fear and Trembling*
C. S. Lewis's *The Abolition of Man*
Alasdair MacIntyre's *After Virtue*
Marcus Aurelius's *Meditations*
Friedrich Nietzsche's *On the Genealogy of Morality*
Friedrich Nietzsche's *Beyond Good and Evil*
Plato's *Republic*
Plato's *Symposium*
Jean-Jacques Rousseau's *The Social Contract*
Gilbert Ryle's *The Concept of Mind*
Baruch Spinoza's *Ethics*
Sun Tzu's *The Art of War*
Ludwig Wittgenstein's *Philosophical Investigations*

POLITICS

Benedict Anderson's *Imagined Communities*
Aristotle's *Politics*
Bernard Bailyn's *The Ideological Origins of the American Revolution*
Edmund Burke's *Reflections on the Revolution in France*
John C. Calhoun's *A Disquisition on Government*
Ha-Joon Chang's *Kicking Away the Ladder*
Hamid Dabashi's *Iran: A People Interrupted*
Hamid Dabashi's *Theology of Discontent: The Ideological Foundation of the Islamic Revolution in Iran*
Robert Dahl's *Democracy and its Critics*
Robert Dahl's *Who Governs?*
David Brion Davis's *The Problem of Slavery in the Age of Revolution*

Alexis De Tocqueville's *Democracy in America*
James Ferguson's *The Anti-Politics Machine*
Frank Dikotter's *Mao's Great Famine*
Sheila Fitzpatrick's *Everyday Stalinism*
Eric Foner's *Reconstruction: America's Unfinished Revolution, 1863-1877*
Milton Friedman's *Capitalism and Freedom*
Francis Fukuyama's *The End of History and the Last Man*
John Lewis Gaddis's *We Now Know: Rethinking Cold War History*
Ernest Gellner's *Nations and Nationalism*
David Graeber's *Debt: the First 5000 Years*
Antonio Gramsci's *The Prison Notebooks*
Alexander Hamilton, John Jay & James Madison's *The Federalist Papers*
Friedrich Hayek's *The Road to Serfdom*
Christopher Hill's *The World Turned Upside Down*
Thomas Hobbes's *Leviathan*
John A. Hobson's *Imperialism: A Study*
Samuel P. Huntington's *The Clash of Civilizations and the Remaking of World Order*
Tony Judt's *Postwar: A History of Europe Since 1945*
David C. Kang's *China Rising: Peace, Power and Order in East Asia*
Paul Kennedy's *The Rise and Fall of Great Powers*
Robert Keohane's *After Hegemony*
Martin Luther King Jr.'s *Why We Can't Wait*
Henry Kissinger's *World Order: Reflections on the Character of Nations and the Course of History*
John Locke's *Two Treatises of Government*
Niccolò Machiavelli's *The Prince*
Thomas Robert Malthus's *An Essay on the Principle of Population*
Mahmood Mamdani's *Citizen and Subject: Contemporary Africa And The Legacy Of Late Colonialism*
Karl Marx's *Capital*
John Stuart Mill's *On Liberty*
John Stuart Mill's *Utilitarianism*
Hans Morgenthau's *Politics Among Nations*
Thomas Paine's *Common Sense*
Thomas Paine's *Rights of Man*
Thomas Piketty's *Capital in the Twenty-First Century*
Robert D. Putman's *Bowling Alone*
John Rawls's *Theory of Justice*
Jean-Jacques Rousseau's *The Social Contract*
Theda Skocpol's *States and Social Revolutions*
Adam Smith's *The Wealth of Nations*
Sun Tzu's *The Art of War*
Henry David Thoreau's *Civil Disobedience*
Thucydides's *The History of the Peloponnesian War*
Kenneth Waltz's *Theory of International Politics*
Max Weber's *Politics as a Vocation*
Odd Arne Westad's *The Global Cold War: Third World Interventions And The Making Of Our Times*

POSTCOLONIAL STUDIES

Roland Barthes's *Mythologies*
Frantz Fanon's *Black Skin, White Masks*
Homi K. Bhabha's *The Location of Culture*
Gustavo Gutiérrez's *A Theology of Liberation*
Edward Said's *Orientalism*
Gayatri Chakravorty Spivak's *Can the Subaltern Speak?*

PSYCHOLOGY

Gordon Allport's *The Nature of Prejudice*
Alan Baddeley & Graham Hitch's *Aggression: A Social Learning Analysis*
Albert Bandura's *Aggression: A Social Learning Analysis*
Leon Festinger's *A Theory of Cognitive Dissonance*
Sigmund Freud's *The Interpretation of Dreams*
Betty Friedan's *The Feminine Mystique*
Michael R. Gottfredson & Travis Hirschi's *A General Theory of Crime*
Eric Hoffer's *The True Believer: Thoughts on the Nature of Mass Movements*
William James's *Principles of Psychology*
Elizabeth Loftus's *Eyewitness Testimony*
A. H. Maslow's *A Theory of Human Motivation*
Stanley Milgram's *Obedience to Authority*
Steven Pinker's *The Better Angels of Our Nature*
Oliver Sacks's *The Man Who Mistook His Wife For a Hat*
Richard Thaler & Cass Sunstein's *Nudge: Improving Decisions About Health, Wealth and Happiness*
Amos Tversky's *Judgment under Uncertainty: Heuristics and Biases*
Philip Zimbardo's *The Lucifer Effect*

SCIENCE

Rachel Carson's *Silent Spring*
William Cronon's *Nature's Metropolis: Chicago And The Great West*
Alfred W. Crosby's *The Columbian Exchange*
Charles Darwin's *On the Origin of Species*
Richard Dawkin's *The Selfish Gene*
Thomas Kuhn's *The Structure of Scientific Revolutions*
Geoffrey Parker's *Global Crisis: War, Climate Change and Catastrophe in the Seventeenth Century*
Mathis Wackernagel & William Rees's *Our Ecological Footprint*

SOCIOLOGY

Michelle Alexander's *The New Jim Crow: Mass Incarceration in the Age of Colorblindness*
Gordon Allport's *The Nature of Prejudice*
Albert Bandura's *Aggression: A Social Learning Analysis*
Hanna Batatu's *The Old Social Classes And The Revolutionary Movements Of Iraq*
Ha-Joon Chang's *Kicking Away the Ladder*
W. E. B. Du Bois's *The Souls of Black Folk*
Émile Durkheim's *On Suicide*
Frantz Fanon's *Black Skin, White Masks*
Frantz Fanon's *The Wretched of the Earth*
Eric Foner's *Reconstruction: America's Unfinished Revolution, 1863-1877*
Eugene Genovese's *Roll, Jordan, Roll: The World the Slaves Made*
Jack Goldstone's *Revolution and Rebellion in the Early Modern World*
Antonio Gramsci's *The Prison Notebooks*
Richard Herrnstein & Charles A Murray's *The Bell Curve: Intelligence and Class Structure in American Life*
Eric Hoffer's *The True Believer: Thoughts on the Nature of Mass Movements*
Jane Jacobs's *The Death and Life of Great American Cities*
Robert Lucas's *Why Doesn't Capital Flow from Rich to Poor Countries?*
Jay Macleod's *Ain't No Makin' It: Aspirations and Attainment in a Low Income Neighborhood*
Elaine May's *Homeward Bound: American Families in the Cold War Era*
Douglas McGregor's *The Human Side of Enterprise*
C. Wright Mills's *The Sociological Imagination*

Thomas Piketty's *Capital in the Twenty-First Century*
Robert D. Putman's *Bowling Alone*
David Riesman's *The Lonely Crowd: A Study of the Changing American Character*
Edward Said's *Orientalism*
Joan Wallach Scott's *Gender and the Politics of History*
Theda Skocpol's *States and Social Revolutions*
Max Weber's *The Protestant Ethic and the Spirit of Capitalism*

THEOLOGY

Augustine's *Confessions*
Benedict's *Rule of St Benedict*
Gustavo Gutiérrez's *A Theology of Liberation*
Carole Hillenbrand's *The Crusades: Islamic Perspectives*
David Hume's *Dialogues Concerning Natural Religion*
Immanuel Kant's *Religion within the Boundaries of Mere Reason*
Ernst Kantorowicz's *The King's Two Bodies: A Study in Medieval Political Theology*
Søren Kierkegaard's *The Sickness Unto Death*
C. S. Lewis's *The Abolition of Man*
Saba Mahmood's *The Politics of Piety: The Islamic Revival and the Feminist Subject*
Baruch Spinoza's *Ethics*
Keith Thomas's *Religion and the Decline of Magic*

COMING SOON

Chris Argyris's *The Individual and the Organisation*
Seyla Benhabib's *The Rights of Others*
Walter Benjamin's *The Work Of Art in the Age of Mechanical Reproduction*
John Berger's *Ways of Seeing*
Pierre Bourdieu's *Outline of a Theory of Practice*
Mary Douglas's *Purity and Danger*
Roland Dworkin's *Taking Rights Seriously*
James G. March's *Exploration and Exploitation in Organisational Learning*
Ikujiro Nonaka's *A Dynamic Theory of Organizational Knowledge Creation*
Griselda Pollock's *Vision and Difference*
Amartya Sen's *Inequality Re-Examined*
Susan Sontag's *On Photography*
Yasser Tabbaa's *The Transformation of Islamic Art*
Ludwig von Mises's *Theory of Money and Credit*

Macat Disciplines

Access the greatest ideas and thinkers across entire disciplines, including

Postcolonial Studies

Roland Barthes's *Mythologies*
Frantz Fanon's *Black Skin, White Masks*
Homi K. Bhabha's *The Location of Culture*
Gustavo Gutiérrez's *A Theology of Liberation*
Edward Said's *Orientalism*
Gayatri Chakravorty Spivak's *Can the Subaltern Speak?*

Macat analyses are available from all good bookshops and libraries.

Access hundreds of analyses through one, multimedia tool.
Join free for one month **library.macat.com**

Macat Disciplines

Access the greatest ideas and thinkers across entire disciplines, including

FEMINISM, GENDER AND QUEER STUDIES

Simone De Beauvoir's
The Second Sex

Michel Foucault's
History of Sexuality

Betty Friedan's
The Feminine Mystique

Saba Mahmood's
The Politics of Piety: The Islamic Revival and the Feminist Subject

Joan Wallach Scott's
Gender and the Politics of History

Mary Wollstonecraft's
A Vindication of the Rights of Woman

Virginia Woolf's
A Room of One's Own

Judith Butler's
Gender Trouble

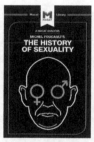

Macat analyses are available from all good bookshops and libraries.

Access hundreds of analyses through one, multimedia tool.
Join free for one month **library.macat.com**

Printed in the United States
by Baker & Taylor Publisher Services